YORK NOTES

ROMEO AND JULIET

WILLIAM SHAKESPEARE

NOTES BY N.H. KEEBLE

  Longman

 York Press

Exterior picture of the Globe Theatre reproduced by permission of the
Raymond Mander and Joe Mitchenson Theatre Collection
Reconstruction of the Globe Theatre interior reprinted from Hodges,
The Globe Restored (1968) by permission of Oxford University Press

YORK PRESS
322 Old Brompton Road, London SW5 9JH

PEARSON EDUCATION LIMITED
Edinburgh Gate, Harlow,
Essex CM20 2JE, United Kingdom
Associated companies, branches and representatives throughout the world

First published 1998
This new and fully revised edition first published 2004
11 10

ISBN: 978-0-582-82307-5

Designed by Michelle Cannatella
Typeset by Pantek Arts Ltd, Maidstone, Kent
Printed in China
(EPC/10)

CONTENTS

PART FOUR

CRITICAL HISTORY

PART FIVE

PART ONE

INTRODUCTION

HOW TO STUDY A PLAY

Studying on your own requires self-discipline and a carefully thought-out work plan in order to be effective.

- Drama is a special kind of writing (the technical term is 'genre') because it needs a performance in the theatre to arrive at a full interpretation of its meaning. Try to imagine that you are a member of the audience when reading the play. Think about how it could be presented on the stage, not just about the words on the page.

CHECK THE BOOK

For a guide to the meanings of words used by Shakespeare, see C.T. Onions, *A Shakespeare Glossary*.

- Drama is always about conflict of some sort (which may be below the surface). Identify the conflicts in the play and you will be close to identifying the large ideas or themes which bind all the parts together.

- Make careful notes on themes, character, plot and any sub-plots of the play.

- Why do you like or dislike the characters in the play? How do your feelings towards them develop and change?

- Playwrights find non-realistic ways of allowing an audience to see into the minds and motives of their characters, for example **soliloquy**, aside or music. Consider how such dramatic devices are used in the play you are studying.

- Think of the playwright writing the play. Why were these particular arrangements of events, characters and speeches chosen?

- Cite exact sources for all quotations, whether from the text itself or from critical commentaries. Wherever possible find your own examples from the play to back up your opinions.

- Always express your ideas in your own words.

These York Notes offer an introduction to *Romeo and Juliet* and cannot substitute for close reading of the text and the study of secondary sources.

READING *ROMEO AND JULIET*

Romeo and Juliet is amongst the most famous of Shakespeare's plays. Since its first performance at the end of the sixteenth century it has been a constant presence in our culture, referred to in countless books. It has been reworked in opera, ballet, film, music and fiction. Through his depiction of their fate Shakespeare created one of the icons of our culture and raised Romeo and Juliet to rank beside Lancelot and Guinevere, Tristan and Iseult, as doomed lovers caught up in one of the three great tragic love stories of the western world. Many who have never even read a word of Shakespeare will recognise their names, and there can hardly be an educated person in the English-speaking world who has not heard of the feud between Montagues and Capulets and of this ill-fated love story.

The self-destructive passion of lovers at odds with the expectations and obligations of the world in which they live is at the heart of two of Shakespeare's tragedies. *Romeo and Juliet* is distinguished from the other (*Antony and Cleopatra*) as a tragedy of *young* love. Its extraordinary power has much to do with the way it recreates the passionate extremism of youth, the excess of its hopes and its despairs, the clash between its idealism and the bitterness of experienced adults. It captures both, on the one hand, the innocence of youth, confident it can overcome (or ignore) the world and, on the other, its passionate self-centredness, its determination to count no cost in seeking the satisfaction of its desire. As the poet John Donne succinctly put it in a poem probably written at the same time as this play, the world of their love is so self-sufficient that for Romeo and Juliet, wholly absorbed in each other, 'Nothing else is' ('The Sun Rising'). That is both the splendour and the tragedy of their story.

> **CONTEXT**
>
> The stirring symphony, *Romeo and Juliet* (1839) by the French composer Hector Berlioz, was inspired by Shakespeare's play.

And yet, for all the power of its depiction of adolescent passion in conflict with a world riven by partisan hatred, materialism and hypocrisy, it is not easy for a modern reader to get on terms with this play. It fails to meet many of the expectations which we bring to a text and many of its features can appear strange, even slightly silly. For this there are three reasons: first, the nature of the stage for which Shakespeare wrote; secondly, the conventions and style of Elizabethan literature; thirdly, the passage of time and changes in the English language since the play's composition.

Because of these features the text presents modern readers with many questions which make it difficult to respond positively to the play. Why, for example, is the action so improbable, so unrealistic? Why is the language so ornate? How are we to believe in these characters? If they are supposed to be Italians, why do they sound so English?

It is the purpose of these Notes to answer some of these questions and to discuss some of these difficulties, and so to clear the way to an appreciation of the play and an understanding of why it should hold such a central place in our literary history. We shall consider not only questions of form and style but also the larger issues raised by the text: discussion of why Romeo and Juliet die, for example, leads to reflection on the nature of tragedy. Their fate raises questions about the duty of children, of parents, of families, of the Church and of the State. The suddenness of their love, others' views of it and the difficulties it encounters prompt questions about the nature of love and of sexual desire. Examination of these and other aspects of the play is intended to help the reader to experience the affective power of Shakespeare's poetry and the deeply moving, but also deeply perplexing, tragic world of his play.

 CHECK THE NET
http://web.uvic.ca/ shakespeare/ lists sites useful for the study of Shakespeare.

PART TWO

SUMMARIES

A NOTE ON THE TEXT

Romeo and Juliet was published in a quarto in 1597 and again in 1599 (these two editions are distinguished as Q1 and Q2). Q1 is a bad quarto: it prints the text of the play as two or three of the actors who took part in a performance remembered it. Such a memorised version is obviously unreliable. But although Q1 is short and often confused, it does reflect an actual performance of Shakespeare's time. It has unusually full stage directions and must often record what the actors actually said and did on the stage. (Q1 is printed as an appendix in H.H. Furness, ed., *Romeo and Juliet*, New Variorum Edition of Shakespeare, NY, 1963.)

Q2, on the other hand, is based upon a written copy of the play, but although it is fuller and more reliable than Q1, it still has many errors. For example, the four lines II.2.188–91 are printed not only there but again at the beginning of the Friar's speech which opens II.3. A modern editor has to decide where he or she thinks Shakespeare meant them to be. Nor does Q2 always make clear who is speaking: the parts of the musicians at the end of IV.5, for example, are not clearly distinguished.

It may even have been Shakespeare's own manuscript that the printer of Q2 worked with, for quite often it prints what appears to be a rough draft of lines, followed by a second version. For example, I.2.14 and 15 look like two versions of the same line.

Or again, in Romeo's long speech to the Friar in III.3, lines 40–4 repeat themselves, using almost the same words. Almost certainly, Shakespeare did not intend this repetition, and it looks as though the printer did not notice that one of the lines had been crossed out.

One passage of a play does exist in Shakespeare's handwriting. This is his contribution of nearly 150 lines to *Sir Thomas More*, a play by other dramatists. This passage is printed in the editions of

CHECK THE BOOK

The Q1 version of *Romeo and Juliet* has recently been printed in facsimile by the Malone Society (2000).

Shakespeare's *Complete Works*, edited by Peter Alexander, London, 1951, and by Stanley Wells and Gary Taylor, Oxford, 1988. A glance at it will show the kind of difficulties the printer of Q2 probably dealt with: spelling, corrections, line and speech divisions all present problems in this manuscript as Shakespeare left it.

A third edition (Q3, 1609) was based on Q2, and so were a fourth (Q4, 1622) and a fifth (Q5, 1637). These texts contain some corrections of errors in Q2, but we cannot know if they were simply the printer's guesses or were actually what Shakespeare wrote. Besides, they carried on many of the old errors, and added new ones of their own. The Folio text of 1623 was based on Q3. Modern editors therefore work with Q1 and Q2 as the earliest versions on which all the others are based. They will make Q2 their main text (as the fuller version), and check it against Q1 when they suspect an error. They will also see if later versions offer a possible correction in such cases.

As an example of the difficulties, take the variation in only one word in the printed texts. Romeo addresses Juliet in II.2.167. What he says appears like this in the different editions:

Madame? (Q1)

My Neece? (Q2, Q3, F1)

My Deere? (Q4, Q5)

My Sweet? (F2, F3, F4)

In the New Penguin edition, 'neece' is preferred and spelled 'nyas', but other modern editors print 'sweet'. When there are so many choices over a single word, it is clear that modern editions of the complete texts will vary considerably from each other.

These notes take as their text the New Penguin Shakespeare edition of the play, edited by T. J. B. Spencer, Penguin, 1967, and frequently reprinted thereafter. This has an excellent introduction, and very full

CHECK THE NET
http://www.
shakespeare.org.uk/
is a comprehensive
Shakespearean site.

and helpful notes in the commentary which follows the text. There is also a discussion of the textual problems of the play. Other available paperback editions are given in **Further Reading**.

SYNOPSIS

In Act I Romeo, infatuated by Rosaline (whom we never meet), goes to the party given by Lord Capulet on Sunday evening in order to see her. There he meets Juliet and, forgetting Rosaline, falls in love with her (I.5). However, the Act ends with the lovers discovering each other's identity, and hence the threatening fact that, as Juliet is a Capulet and Romeo a Montague, they belong to feuding families who would never let them see each other. In Act II the course of their love nevertheless moves quickly. That night, in the famous balcony scene (II.2), they exchange vows, and the following afternoon they are married secretly by Friar Laurence (II.6).

In Act III the tragic counter-movement begins. Romeo had not been invited to Lord Capulet's party, and the Capulet Tybalt is determined not to let his intrusion pass unpunished. In the quarrel and fight that follow in the first scene of Act III Romeo's friend Mercutio is killed by Tybalt and Romeo avenges his friend's death by killing Tybalt. For this, Romeo is banished from Verona by the Prince, Escalus. The Friar advises Romeo to leave Verona to live in the nearby city of Mantua until there is an opportunity to proclaim his marriage to Juliet publicly (III.2), and so, after spending Monday night with Juliet, Romeo leaves (III.5). Juliet's parents mistake her sorrow at Romeo's leaving for grief for her dead cousin, Tybalt, and think to overcome it by insisting that on the next Thursday she should marry her suitor, Count Paris (III.4). This Juliet refuses to do, and her father threatens never to see her again if she persists in this disobedience (III.5).

At the beginning of Act IV Juliet seeks the advice of Friar Laurence. He suggests that the night before her marriage she should take a potion which will make her appear dead on her wedding morning. She would then be placed in the family vault, from which he and Romeo could rescue her when she awakens, and Romeo could take

> **CONTEXT**
>
> In 1830 the Italian composer Vincenzo Bellini wrote an opera entitled *I Capuleti e I Montecchi* (*The Capulets and the Montagues*), based on *Romeo and Juliet*.

CHECK THE FILM

Baz Lurhmann's wonderfully inventive 1997 film version of *Romeo + Juliet*, starring Claire Danes and Leonardo DiCaprio, set the play in a modern, but fantasy, Veronese setting.

her back to live with him in Mantua. To this she agrees, and so submits to her father who, overjoyed at this change of heart, brings the wedding forward to the next day, Wednesday (IV.2). The Friar meanwhile writes to Romeo to tell him of the scheme and bids him return from Mantua. However, while all else goes according to plan, this letter is never delivered (V.2). Instead, Romeo is told by his servant that Juliet is really dead (V.1). On hearing the news, Romeo returns to the Capulet vault, where Juliet lies, there to poison himself. When Juliet wakes up in the vault, and sees Romeo's body, she stabs herself in her grief. The deaths of both their heirs, explained by Friar Laurence in a summary of the plot (V.3.229–69), reconcile the Capulet and Montague families.

DETAILED SUMMARIES

PROLOGUE

- The Chorus introduces the matter of the play in a **sonnet** addressed to the audience.
- It tells of the feud between two Veronese families and how the tragic love affair between two young people finally mends the feud.

The first four lines (or **quatrain**) prepare the audience to see the long-standing hostility between two equally noble Veronese families (the Capulets and Montagues) breaking out anew; the second quatrain foretells the healing of this feud through the deaths of a pair of ill-fated lovers, children of these families (Romeo and Juliet). This is to be the matter of the play, which will last two hours. The Chorus's concluding two lines (or **couplet**) asks the audience to watch with patience while the actors do their best to please them.

CONTEXT

The Chorus was a feature of Classical drama which was adapted and adopted by Renaissance dramatists. Shakespeare makes only occasional use of the figure. Other examples occur in *Henry V* and in *The Winter's Tale*.

COMMENTARY

The Chorus's introduction stresses the tragic nature of the play – we are not prepared by him for the comic figure of the Nurse or the wit of Mercutio. Although the word *chorus* is taken from Classical drama, where the Chorus consists of a group of characters commenting upon the action, the Chorus here (as in such other Shakespeare plays as *Henry V, Henry VIII* and *Troilus and Cressida*) is a single figure.

**CHECK
THE FILM**
In his film
Romeo + Juliet,
Baz Luhrmann
has the prologue
spoken as a news
bulletin on a TV
screen.

GLOSSARY	
1	**dignity** noble rank
3	**mutiny** violent quarrelling
4	**civil** belonging to citizens and civilised
6	**star-crossed** thwarted by the influence of the stars, ill-fated
7	**misadventured** tragic
12	**traffic** business
14	**miss** be wanting, seem to be inadequate in our performance

ACT I

SCENE 1

- The feud between Montagues and Capulets, and Romeo's love for Rosaline, are introduced.

Time: 9 a.m. Sunday morning (I.1.160–1) (How the day is discovered is explained in Time in the Play.)

Benvolio, a Montague, tries to stop a quarrel between Capulet and Montague servants, but is taunted to fight in earnest with Tybalt, a Capulet. The uproar caused by Veronese citizens joining in the fray brings Lord and Lady Capulet and Lord and Lady Montague to the scene and, finally, the Prince of Verona, Escalus, who commands peace and decrees that any further fighting between the two families will be punished by death.

CONTEXT
The Italian city of
Verona is the scene
for the early part
of Shakespeare's
comedy *Two
Gentlemen of
Verona* and it is
the home of
Petruchio, the hero
of *The Taming of
the Shrew.*

When the stage is cleared, Benvolio explains to Montague how the fight began. We then learn of Romeo's strangely solitary habits and depressed mood, which his father, Montague, is unable to understand. As Romeo enters, Benvolio resolves to discover what troubles him. Romeo admits he is sad because the lady he loves does not return his affection. Should he, as Benvolio advises, try to forget her by seeking out other women, their appearance would only emphasise how much the beauty of the woman he loves excels theirs.

COMMENTARY

The play begins like a comedy, with the boastful and bawdy exchanges of the Capulet servants Sampson and Gregory who, meeting Abram and another Montague servant, embark on a quarrel with them which their evident lack of heroism renders comic. Through the comedy of the servants aping their social betters, the play mocks the seriousness with which Montagues and Capulets take their feud and alerts the audience to the absurdity of their obsession. In their case, however, it will prove tragic.

GLOSSARY	
1	**carry coals** a dirty task performed by the lowest servants; proverbially, to put up with being humiliated
2	**colliers** coal merchants; colloquial term of abuse
3	**choler** anger; pun on 'collier'
3	**draw** draw our swords
4	**collar** hangman's noose; pun on 'collier' and 'choler'
5	**moved** aroused, angered
8–9	**To move ... art moved** Gregory now uses 'move' literally, and so means that in a quarrel Sampson would run, not hold his ground and fight
10	**dog** worthless fellow
11	**take the wall** walk along the side of the path next to a building (and thus avoid the mess in the gutters and rubbish thrown from windows above); Sampson is boasting that he would not step aside for any Montague
12–13	**For the weakest ... wall** Gregory turns Sampson's boast against him by using a proverb which again uses 'wall' but means that the less powerful are pushed aside by the stronger
15	**weaker vessels** Elizabethan thinking generally assumed that woman was inferior to man and used this biblical phrase (I Peter 3:7) to express the idea
15	**thrust** Sampson applies Gregory's words to women, who are pushed against the wall by their lovers
21	**civil** Sampson is being **ironic**

CHECK THE FILM

In Franco Zeffirelli's film of *Romeo and Juliet* the 'civil brawl' of I.1 develops into a full-scale city riot.

GLOSSARY

24–5 maidenhead virginity

25 sense meaning

26 sense feeling

27 stand have an erection

29 fish (slang) women

30 poor-John hake, a kind of fish, dried and salted, eaten by poor people

35 Fear me not do not be afraid for me, on my account; in the next line Gregory takes the words in the sense 'do not be afraid of me'

36 marry (mild exclamation) By the Virgin Mary

40 list please

41 I will bite ... thumb insulting gesture such as might provoke a quarrel

57–8 Here comes one ... kinsmen Gregory, a Capulet servant, must mean Tybalt, though a Montague, Benvolio, enters first

62 washing slashing

64 What, art thou drawn have you your sword out

64 heartless hinds a pun on female deer ('hinds') without their stags ('harts'), meaning cowardly ('heartless') women servants ('hinds')

72 bills, and partisans kinds of pikes

79 Hold me not Montague speaks to his wife, as is clear from the next line

82 Profaners misusers

82 neighbour-stainèd stained with the blood of neighbours

87 mistempered wrongly made ('tempered') because you use them in bad temper

89 airy vague; this is all we hear of the cause of the quarrel between Capulets and Montagues

95 Cankered with peace grown rusty through lack of use

95 cankered hate malignant hate

97 pay ... peace pay the penalty for breaking the peace

104 new abroach newly open

114 on part and part on one side or the other

120 drive drove

127 most sought ... be found wanted above all to be where fewest people might be found

CHECK THE FILM

In Baz Luhrmann's *Romeo + Juliet*, the Prince appears as Captain Prince, Chief of Police, who patrols the city in a helicopter.

CHECK THE NET

http://www.online-literature.com/ provides a searchable online text for *Romeo and Juliet* which allows you to locate any reference or word.

GLOSSARY		
129	**humour** inclination	
136	**Aurora** goddess of dawn	
137	**heavy** sad	
138	**pens** shuts	
141	**portentous** ominous	
141	**humour** mood	
145	**by any means** in every way possible	
149	**close** reserved	
150	**sounding** fathoming, being understood (literally, 'measured')	
151	**envious** malicious	
159	**shrift** confession	
161	**But new** only just	
164	**makes** would make	
169	**view** appearance; Benvolio thinks of Cupid, god of love	
171	**muffled** Cupid was often depicted with eyes covered, to signify that love is blind	
171	**still** always	
177	**create** created; Romeo, trying in vain to describe his feelings, in frustration calls on 'anything', the first thing that God created from nothing, for example	
183	**coz** cousin	
187	**propagate** increase	
193	**discreet** discriminating	
194	**A choking ... sweet** a poison which chokes (the life out of you) and a preserved sweet (which is delicious and desirable)	
195	**Soft** go softly, that is, wait a moment	
199	**sadness** earnest	
200	**groan** Romeo takes 'sadness' in the sense of 'sorrow'	
205	**aimed so near** guessed as much	
206	**fair** easily seen; a play on 'fair', meaning beautiful, in the preceding line	
209	**Cupid's arrow** anyone pierced by an arrow Cupid's bow would fall in love	
209	**Dian's wit** the cleverness and skill of Diana, goddess of chastity, who will preserve herself from Romeo's amorous advances	

> **GLOSSARY**
>
> | | | |
> |---|---|---|
> | 212 | **stay** | submit to, endure |
> | 214 | **ope** | open |
> | 214 | **lap** | (euphemism) Romeo wishes her to open her legs for sexual intercourse |
> | 216 | **store** | wealth |
> | 218 | **in that sparing … waste** | because, abstaining from sex, she will deprive the future of her offspring |
> | 219 | **starved** | killed |
> | 228 | **beauties** | beautiful women |
> | 229 | **in question** | to mind |
> | 230 | **masks** | ladies of rank would wear masks at public festivities |
> | 234 | **passing** | surpassing, exceptionally |
> | 235 | **note** | reminder |
> | 238 | **pay** | pay you for that, that is, Benvolio will teach Romeo to forget |
> | 238 | **die in debt** | die with payment unmade, die in the attempt |

SCENE 2

- Count Paris is to attend the Capulet's party to see his intended Juliet.
- Romeo and Benvolio decide to gatecrash the party in order to see Rosaline.

Time: Sunday afternoon (I.1.100; 2.1–2)

Count Paris appears for the first time and asks Capulet for permission to marry his daughter (Juliet). Capulet hesitates, because Juliet is so young, but says he would agree if Juliet consents. Inviting Paris to the feast that is to be held that night, Capulet advises him to look at the ladies there to be sure it is Juliet whom he would like to marry. As the servant whom Capulet directs to invite his guests cannot read their names on the list he is given, he asks Romeo, who has entered with Benvolio, to read them for him. Rosaline, the lady Romeo loves, is one of the guests: because of this, Romeo and Benvolio decide to go to the feast, although they have

CHECK THE FILM

In Baz Luhrmann's *Romeo + Juliet*, Paris appears on the cover of *Time* magazine as 'Dave Paris, Bachelor of the Year'.

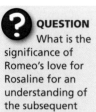

QUESTION
What is the significance of Romeo's love for Rosaline for an understanding of the subsequent development of the play?

not been invited. Benvolio hopes to show Romeo that Rosaline cannot equal the beauty of the other ladies present; Romeo wants simply to see Rosaline.

COMMENTARY

The character of Rosaline plays no part in the play. Shakespeare wants the audience's attention to be focused solely on Romeo and Juliet. To introduce Rosaline and develop Romeo's relationship with her on stage would be to distract the audience from the main love story.

GLOSSARY	
sd	*County* count
1	**bound** bound to keep the peace (following the quarrel in Act I.1)
4	**reckoning** reputation
6	**suit** wooing, request to marry
14	**hopes** hopes for the future, that is, children
17	**My will … but a part** my desire for her to agree is only part of the matter (Paris has to get Juliet's consent as well)
18	**she agreed** when once she has agreed
18	**within … choice** according to what she chooses
19	**according** agreeing
20	**accustomed** customary, traditional
22	**store** company
25	**Earth-treading stars** young ladies so beautiful they seem to be stars that have come down to earth
30	**Inherit** receive
32	**mine** my daughter (Juliet)
33	**May stand … none** may count as one of the crowd though amongst so many hardly noticeable, and not equal to the others ('reckoning' meaning both 'counting' and 'assessment')
34	**sirrah** a word used by gentlemen to their inferiors
34	**trudge** walk (without the sense of weary effort the word has in modern English)
37	**stay** wait
39–41	**It is written … nets** (proverbs) you should stick to what you know how to do. But the servant muddles them all up
41–3	**But I am sent … here writ** literacy at this date was confined to the professions and some of the upper classes

GLOSSARY

47	**holp**	helped
48	**cures … another's languish**	is cured by languishing for someone else (or, perhaps, by making someone else languish)
51	**plantain leaf**	Romeo takes the 'infection' of line 49 literally, and so wittily suggests a herbal remedy; plantain, a common English weed was used to cure infection and staunch blood
57	**God gi' good-e'en**	God give you good evening
79	**crush**	drink
82	**Rosaline**	the first time Romeo's beloved is named
84	**unattainted**	unprejudiced, impartial
89	**these**	these eyes of mine
94	**poised**	balanced, weighed
98	**scant**	scarcely
100	**my own**	my own as belonging to my lady

SCENE 3

- Juliet is informed of her arranged marriage to Paris.
- She is prepared by her mother to look out for Paris at the party.

Time: later on Sunday afternoon (I.3.81)

Constantly interrupted by the Nurse, Lady Capulet tells Juliet that Paris wants to marry her, and advises her to take careful note of how handsome he is at the feast that night. Juliet agrees to see if she likes him.

CONTEXT

Aptly, given her name, Juliet's birthday falls in July.

COMMENTARY

In this, Juliet's first appearance, she is submissive and obedient to her parents (see especially lines 98–100); when she has fallen in love she will discover a new independence of mind. The Nurse's words at the opening of this scene are echoed when (with very different consequences) Lady Capulet again sends her to fetch Juliet in IV.5.1–4.

GLOSSARY

2	**by my maidenhead ... twelve** the implication is that by thirteen the Nurse had no maidenhead to swear by
4	**God forbid** that is, God forbid that anything should have happened to her as she does not come
8	**give leave awhile** leave us alone for a while
10	**thou's ... counsel** thou shalt hear our private talk
14	**teen** sorrow
16	**Lammastide** 1 August, a harvest festival
16	**odd** a few (in the next line the Nurse takes the word in its modern sense)
20	**Susan** the Nurse's daughter
24	**earthquake** earthquakes were regarded by Elizabethan's as ominous portents
27	**wormwood** a bitter-tasting plant
27	**dug** nipple; the Nurse suckled Juliet (it was common for noble ladies to have 'wet nurses' for their babies); the wormwood was to wean the baby
30	**I ... brain** I can remember
32	**fool** used as a term of affection here
34	**Shake ... dovehouse** the Nurse personifies the dovehouse and its reaction to the earthquake
34	**trow** believe
35	**To bid me trudge** to tell me to go (because of the earthquake)
37	**high-lone** all alone, by herself
37	**th'rood** the cross of Christ
41	**'A** he
43	**fall backward** a bawdy suggestion that when she is older Juliet will lie on her back under a man
44	**holidam** holiness; a common exclamation
49	**it stinted** she stopped
53	**it ... it** she ... her
54	**stone** testicle
66	**dispositions** the sense is singular, disposition, inclination
77	**man of wax** a model, that is, perfect man
84	**married lineament** harmonious feature (of his face)
85	**one ... content** each suits the other, so making a perfect whole
87	**margent** margin; throughout this speech Lady Capulet compares Paris's face to a book

CHECK THE FILM

The film *West Side Story* (1961), directed by Robert Wise with choreography by Jerome Robbins, starring Natalie Wood and Richard Beymer, transfers the plot of *Romeo and Juliet* to 1950s Upper West Side, New York.

CHECK THE BOOK
For comment on this all-female scene, see Dympna Callaghan's essay, 'The Ideology of Romantic Love' in Callaghan, ed., *Weyward Sisters: Shakespeare and Feminist Politics,*1994.

GLOSSARY

89	**only lacks a cover** needs only the embrace of a wife (as 'cover' of his 'book')
90–1	**The fish ... hide** the sense is that just as fish live in the sea so a fair man (Paris) needs a fair wife (Juliet)
96	**bigger** i.e., when pregnant
99	**endart** dart, pierce
102–3	**Nurse cursed** the Nurse is cursed (for not being there to help)
103	**in extremity** in dire need of help
104	**wait** serve at table
104	**straight** straightaway, immediately
106	**happy ... days** the Nurse thinks of the sexual joy with which a married woman can end the day

SCENE 4

- Benvolio and Mercutio want to go to the party, but Romeo hesitates, having had a dream portending death.
- Romeo's misgivings about attending the Capulet party are overcome by Mercutio.

Time: Sunday evening (I.2.20, 81–100; I.3.81)

Romeo, his cousin Benvolio and his friend Mercutio – a kinsman of the Prince (III.1.109, 145, 188–9; V.3.295) who now appears for the first time – discuss whether to go into Capulet's feast. Although Benvolio and Romeo have not been invited – Mercutio is included amongst the guests on the servant's list (I.2.64–9) – it was quite usual for uninvited maskers to join such parties, and Benvolio is all for going in. Romeo, however, does not care to dance, and, because of a dream, fears something awful – perhaps even his death – will result if they do go in. But Mercutio makes light of his fears, and they enter.

COMMENTARY

This scene adds little to the action, but it introduces a note of foreboding just as Romeo is to meet Juliet for the first time, and it introduces the important character of Mercutio.

CHECK THE BOOK

Mercutio's Queen Mab speech conjures up the fairy world of Shakespeare's *A Midsummer Night's Dream*, a comedy of young love and parental opposition written at about the same time as *Romeo and Juliet*.

CHECK THE FILM

Two silent film versions of *Romeo and Juliet* were produced as early as 1916.

GLOSSARY

sd   maskers people wearing masks on their faces; although *masked balls* (or dances), fashionable at this time, should not be confused with *masques*, dramatic entertainments involving music and dancing, improvised masques could easily be presented by people in masks and costumes at such a party as Capulet's

1   What ... our excuse shall we introduce ourselves and excuse our intrusion; it was customary for maskers to present themselves, often with a formal speech – see, for example, Shakespeare's *Love's Labour's Lost*, V.2.158–69, and *Henry VIII*, Act I.4.65–72

3   The date ... prolixity such speeches ('prolixity') are out of fashion ('date')

4   Cupid maskers would often send a boy, dressed as Cupid, to introduce them – see, for example, Shakespeare's *Timon of Athens*, Act I.2.117–22

4   hoodwinked blindfolded

5   Tartar's ... of lath Cupid's wooden bow, from which he loosed his arrows of love, was shaped like a lip, unlike the curved English bow; Shakespeare thought this may have been a Tartar shape from central Asia (although it is in fact Grecian) or, more probably, used 'Tartar' vaguely to mean 'Eastern'

6   crowkeeper scarecrow

7   without-book memorised

9   measure us ... will judge us as they like

10   measure them a measure dance one dance for them

11   torch torchbearers would not join in the dancing

11   ambling dancing (a contemptuous term)

16   stakes fixes

18–21   bound ... bound ... bound (pun) height ... tied ... leap

21   pitch height

29   case mask

30   A visor for a visor mask for an ugly face

31   quote notice

34   betake his legs take to his legs in dancing

36   rushes these were strewn on the floor

37   proverbed ... phrase supported (in what I wish to do) by an old proverb that the onlooker sees the best of the game

39   game that is, here, dancing

GLOSSARY

39   **ne'er so fair** never so good (as now); there was a proverbial saying that one should leave the game (gambling) when the game was at its best

40   **dun's the mouse** a quibble on 'done' in line 39; because the mouse is dark ('dun') it is not easily seen, and so, the meaning is 'be quiet', and so unnoticed like the mouse

40   **constable's own word** the constable, or policeman, would bid his companions be quiet when waiting to catch a criminal

41   **Dun** a name for a horse; there was an expression 'Dun in the mire', like the modern 'stick-in-the-mud', someone who will not venture on anything new

43   **burn daylight** waste time; Romeo takes Mercutio literally in the next line

46   **Take ... meaning** take the sense of what I say, don't take me literally

46–7   **for our ... wits** for good sense is five times more apparent in what we mean than in what we say (that is, than in the words which are the result of what we learn through our five senses)

49   **tonight** last night

52   **In bed asleep** in line 51 Mercutio used 'lie' in the sense 'tell an untruth'; Romeo takes it in the sense 'lie down'

53   **Queen Mab** queen of the fairies

55   **agate** a precious stone, often engraved and set in rings

57   **atomies** tiny creatures

62   **spinners** spiders

64   **traces** reins

66   **film** fine thread of cobweb

69   **Pricked ... maid** there was a saying that, when maids were idle, worms grew in their fingers

78   **suit** petition (which a courtier would present to the king for a fee)

79   **tithe-pig** a pig due to the parish priest who received the tenth part (or 'tithe') of the agricultural produce of his parish

81   **benefice** position in the church held by a parish priest, for which he received payment

84   **ambuscados** ambushes

84   **Spanish blades** Spain was famous for the quality of its swords

85   **healths** drinks (from the expression 'drink to your health')

CHECK THE FILM

In Zeffirelli's film of *Romeo and Juliet*, Mercutio's Queen Mab speech becomes an emotionally charged expression of inner turmoil and disquiet.

GLOSSARY

90	**bakes** matts, tangles together in a hard lump
90	**elf-locks** tangled hair was thought to be the work of elves; to untangle it would bring bad luck (line 91)
90	**sluttish** very dirty
92	**hag** wicked, ugly fairy
93	**learns … bear** teaches them first how to bear children; Mercutio in fact means 'teach them how to conceive children' for he is thinking of young women dreaming of sex as a result of Mab's influence
94	**carriage** both 'deportment' and 'the carrying of a child in the womb'
104	**from ourselves** from our purpose
108	**date** time
109	**expire the term** complete the allotted span

SCENE 5

- At the dance Tybalt recognises Romeo as a Montague.
- Romeo and Juliet meet for the first time and fall in love.
- Romeo learns that Juliet is a Capulet, and she learns that he is a Montague.

Time: later Sunday evening (I.2.20, 81–100; I.3.81)

In Capulet's house the servants are busy clearing the hall for the dance to follow the meal. Capulet welcomes the maskers and watches the dance, recollecting with his cousin his own dancing days long ago. Tybalt realises that one of the maskers is a Montague, and is furious at the intrusion. Capulet, identifying Romeo, orders Tybalt to control himself and behave civilly to so fine a youth, but Tybalt resolves that this will not be the end of the matter. Romeo, who does not take part in the dance, has noticed Juliet and is overpowered by her beauty. He approaches her when the dance ends and in the fourteen lines of an English **sonnet** he woos her, they fall in love and kiss. The Nurse interrupts them, and the scene ends with Romeo learning that Juliet is a Capulet, she that Romeo is a Montague – that is, that each loves an enemy.

CHECK THE FILM
Throughout I.5 in Zeffirelli's film of *Romeo and Juliet*, wide-angle shots of the dance are intercut by close-up shots of Tybalt's threatening face, opposing the ominous to the festive.

COMMENTARY

Building on the last lines of I.4, this scene deepens the note of foreboding. The audience is painfully aware of the hostility and resentment surrounding Romeo and Juliet. Their first encounter is thus fraught with the potential for tragedy.

GLOSSARY		
2	**take away** clear away	
3	**trencher** wooden plate	
6	**joint stools** wooden stools	
7	**court-cupboard** sideboard	
8	**marchpane** marzipan	
9	**let … Nell** the servants are to have their own party; Susan and Nell would be their guests	
15	**longer liver** (colloquialism) Death, who will take us all in the end, so let us be merry now	
18	**walk a bout** have a dance	
20	**makes dainty** is coy (in refusing to dance for no very good reason)	
21	**Am I … ye** does what I say affect you	
27	**A hall** clear the room, let us have a hall	
28	**knaves** the servants (the word is used in good humour here)	
28	**turn the tables up** in order to clear the room for dancing	
30	**unlooked-for** because Romeo and his friends were not expected	
37	**Pentecost** Whitsun	
41	**ward** youth under twenty-one years of age	
46	**Ethiop** Ethiopian, strictly, though the word was used of any black African	
48	**shows** appears	
50	**The measure done** when the dance has ended	
51	**rude** rough (physically) and coarse (socially)	
54	**should** must	
55	**slave** not literally, but a term of contempt	
56	**antic face** fantastic or grotesque mask	
57	**fleer** sneer	
58	**solemnity** celebration	

CHECK THE BOOK

On ideas of adolescence in Shakespeare's time, see Ilana Krausman Ben-Amos, *Adolescence and Youth in Early Modern England*, 1984.

CONTEXT

The first full-length ballet devised by the Scottish choreographer Kenneth MacMillan was derived from *Romeo and Juliet* (1965).

GLOSSARY

59	**stock**	parentage, the noble line of a family's descent
66	**portly**	dignified
68	**well-governed**	well mannered
71	**patient**	calm (Capulet does not mean that Tybalt should be patient and wait for another opportunity)
74	**ill-beseeming**	semblance unsuitable appearance
77	**goodman**	a term used to address a yeoman, that is, a person below the rank of gentleman and so an insult to Tybalt (especially when coupled with 'boy')
77	**Go to**	an expression of exasperation
80	**mutiny**	disturbance
81	**You ... cock-a-hoop**	a colloquial expression explained by Capulet's following **ironic** 'You'll be the man!'
83	**saucy**	insolent (the word was then stronger in sense than in modern English)
85	**contrary**	contradict
86	**hearts**	friends (Capulet turns aside to address his guests)
89	**perforce**	compelled
89	**wilful**	eager, determined
92	**seeming**	apparently
93–106	**If I profane... effect I take**	in these lines, which make up a **sonnet**, Shakespeare pursues an elaborate religious conceit (or extended image), likening Romeo's approach to Juliet to that of a pilgrim to the shrine of a saint, and a kiss to a prayer; such use of religious imagery was not unusual in love poetry, but the delicate ingenuity and detail of this example are remarkable; it has added point in that Romeo's name means, in Italian, 'pilgrim to Rome'
98	**mannerly**	proper
99	**saints**	that is, statues of saints
100	**palmer**	a pilgrim who carried a palm leaf to show he had been to Jerusalem; here, a play on the palm of the hand
105	**though grant ... sake**	though they grant what is prayed for, that is, they are 'moved' (persuaded) by prayers, they do not move physically
110	**by th'book**	Juliet either admits she is deeply affected by the kiss, or she draws back and covers her feelings, for the phrase may mean either 'expertly' ('you have learned how') or 'formally' ('you kiss as though following written instructions, without feeling')

GLOSSARY

117	**chinks**	money (because Juliet is the Capulet heir)
118	**dear account**	awful reckoning to pay
118	**My life … debt**	indebted to, dependent on, my foe
122	**banquet**	not the main meal, which was cleared away for the dance, but a light supper
126	**fay**	faith
126	**waxes**	grows
140	**Prodigious**	ominous, monstrous

ACT II

SCENE 1

- The Chorus stresses the family feud.
- Though mocked by his friends, Romeo cannot bear to leave Juliet's house.

Time: Sunday night, immediately after Capulet's party (II.1.3–4)

After the Chorus has summarised the situation, stressing the fact that Romeo and Juliet cannot easily meet because of their families' feud, Romeo enters for a moment, and we hear that he cannot bear to leave the house where Juliet lives. He withdraws as Benvolio and Mercutio enter looking for him. Benvolio thinks he has seen Romeo jump over a wall (which, we learn in II.2, surrounds the Capulet house and garden) and Mercutio, who does not know Romeo now loves Juliet, attempts to provoke him to rejoin them by making fun of, and bawdy remarks about, Romeo's love for Rosaline. But Romeo does not return and the two friends go home to bed without him.

COMMENTARY

This pause in the action increases the audience's expectation of the lovers' next meeting. The parting from his friends enacts the isolation of Romeo and his separation from the familiar world which is the lot of both lovers in the play.

 CHECK THE FILM

In 1936 George Cukor directed a film version of *Romeo and Juliet* starring Norma Shearer as Juliet and Leslie Howard as Romeo.

CHECK THE FILM

Franco Zeffirelli's 1968 film version of *Romeo and Juliet*, starring Olivia Hussey and Leonard Whiting, aims at an authentic Renaissance setting for the action of the play.

GLOSSARY

Chorus now usually omitted in performances since it adds nothing to the action, although it does add intensity to the love plot

1 **old desire** i.e., Romeo's love for Rosaline

2 **young affection** i.e., Romeo's new love for Juliet

3 **fair** fair woman (Rosaline)

4 **matched** compared

7 **supposed** although supposed his enemy as a Capulet, Juliet is not his foe

10 **use to** are accustomed to

14 **Tempering extremities** modifying extremely harsh circumstances

14 **extreme sweet** excess of love

1 **go forward** that is, go forward beyond Juliet's house (and so away from her)

2 **dull earth** Romeo's own body (God created Adam from earth)

2 **centre** three senses combine: (i) earth was thought to be a heavy element which tended down to the centre of the world (because of gravitation, though that was not then understood), and so Romeo, as earth, must go to his centre; (ii) the centre of Romeo's world is Juliet, as she is all to him; (iii) the heart is the centre of man, and, as Juliet has Romeo's heart, he must return to her to find his centre: the sense of all these meanings is that Romeo cannot leave Juliet, the centre of his life

5 **orchard** probably garden, rather than literally an orchard (though this one does have fruit trees in it, see II.2. 108)

6 **conjure** to call up spirits by reciting magic words (Mercutio goes on to make fun of Romeo's love by reciting a mock incantation, made up of lovers' protestations)

11 **gossip Venus** familiar friend Venus, the goddess of love and mother of Cupid

12 **purblind** blind

13 **Abraham Cupid** two senses are possible: (i) the cunning and roguish Cupid, naked but for a loin cloth, is like the 'Abraham men', half-naked beggars and thieves who wandered England – so, 'rascally Cupid'; (ii) the patriarch Abraham in the Old Testament lived to be 175 years old, and Cupid, though a child, was an old god – so 'old Cupid'

13 **trim** accurately

GLOSSARY

14   **King Cophetua** the hero of an old ballad who fell in love with a beggar girl; the point of the **allusion** is that this was an unlikely match, and so Cupid was particularly clever to bring it about

16   **ape is dead** a term of affection; Mercutio means that as Romeo pretends to be dead by not appearing, his ghost must be conjured up

20   **demesnes** domains, that is, Rosaline's sexual parts

24   **raise** conjure up

24   **circle** conjurors worked in a magic circle, but in these lines there is a second bawdy sense, with references to the female ('circle') and aroused male sexual parts ('raise', 'stand'), to the sexual act ('laid') and its aftermath ('down')

31   **consorted** accompanied

31   **humorous** humid and (with reference to Romeo's apparent unfriendliness) moody

34   **medlar** soft, pear-shaped indented fruit, thought to resemble a woman's sexual parts (with a pun on 'meddle', meaning 'to make love')

38   **open-arse** dialect name for medlar, and a reference to a sexually available female body

38   **poppering pear** a kind of pear and a pun on the act of love-making

39   **truckle bed** a small bed, such as a child might use, implying that Mercutio is innocently going to his bed, while Romeo indulges in sexual activity

QUESTION
What is achieved by the play's frequent use of bawdy language and sexual innuendo?

SCENE 2

- Romeo and Juliet avow their love despite their families' hostility.
- Romeo resolves to seek the Friar's assistance to effect their marriage.

Time: Sunday night, immediately following II.1, to dawn on Monday (II.2.1, 176, 188–91)

CHECK THE FILM

With marvellous ingenuity, and an outrageous inversion of tradition, Baz Lurhmann contrives to present the 'balcony scene' in a swimming pool in his *Romeo + Juliet*, with the lovers conducting their dialogue in the water.

Romeo dismisses Mercutio's jokes, and, seeing Juliet at her balcony, adores her beauty. Juliet, not knowing Romeo is below, confesses that she loves him despite the fact that he is a Montague. Romeo speaks to her and, although Juliet is afraid for his life, he remains in the garden and they acknowledge their love. Juliet speaks honestly and frankly of her affection, and freely tells Romeo that if he means what he says and can send word the next day how they may be married, she will readily be his wife. She arranges to send a go-between to Romeo by nine in the morning to learn what plan he has made. When she goes in, Romeo decides to go to see his father confessor, Friar Laurence, for advice on how to bring about the marriage.

COMMENTARY

The love theme of the first part of the play now begins to move quickly to its climax. Although Romeo and Juliet have only just met, by the time the crucial meeting we now see is over, they are planning to marry. It is for the remarkably beautiful treatment of the confession of love in this scene that the play is best remembered. (The quality of the love here celebrated is emphasised by the contrast with Mercutio's bawdy innuendo in the previous scene.)

GLOSSARY	
1	**He jests ... wound** someone who has never been hurt makes light of another's scars: Romeo means that as Mercutio has never been in love he can easily laugh at a lover's sorrows; 'wounded' recalls Cupid and his arrows
7	**Be not her maid** Romeo has likened Juliet to the sun; in not wanting her to be the maid of the virgin goddess of the moon, Diana, he confesses his hope she may accept his love and so cease to be a virgin
8	**vestal livery** spotlessly pure costume
9	**fools** that is, those who remain virgin and unmarried
17	**spheres** in the old astronomy of Ptolemy the stars and planets were thought to revolve around the earth as though in round, transparent tubes, called 'spheres'
17	**they** that is, the stars
33	**wherefore** why; that is, why are you Romeo and a Montague rather than a member of some other family?
39	**though not** even if you were not
46	**owes** owns

GLOSSARY

61	**thee dislike**	offends, displeases, you
64	**the place death**	to be in this place is to risk your life
73	**proof**	protected against, immune
76	**but thou**	unless you, if you do not
78	**wanting of**	if I lacked
88	**Fain would ... form**	gladly would I follow custom (which requires that the woman refuses her lover's address)
89	**compliment**	conventional polite manners, formality: Juliet's determination here to speak plainly of her love, though hardly what would be expected of a young girl alone at night with a man, is a key feature of her character; it contrasts very obviously with Romeo's elaborate imagery (which Juliet interrupts at 1.109)
93	**Jove**	king of the gods in Roman mythology
97	**So thou wilt**	if that will make you
98	**fond**	affectionate and foolish
101	**cunning ... strange**	skill to be aloof or distant, that is, to follow the usual rules of courtship
131	**frank**	generous
143	**bent**	intention, inclination
152	**strife**	urging
156	**Love ... love**	a loved one ... a loved one
159	**tassel-gentle**	tercel-gentle, a male falcon, the most prized by falconers (and so a compliment to Romeo)
160	**Bondage is hoarse**	as a young girl Juliet would not be free to leave the house unaccompanied or to meet a man without a chaperone; hence, she is 'bound' and cannot call out to Romeo for fear of discovery
161	**Echo**	a mythical nymph condemned to repeat the last words anyone spoke to her, who, unable to declare her love for Narcissus, lived alone in a cave until she died of a broken heart, leaving only her voice behind
167	**nyas**	a young hawk which has not yet left the nest to fly (and so Romeo's fitting reply to 'tassel-gentle')
177	**wanton**	mischievous child
179	**gyves**	shackles
191	**Titan's wheels**	in Greek mythology the Titan sun god Hyperion rode across the sky in a chariot
192	**ghostly**	spiritual
193	**dear hap**	dear happening, that is, good fortune

www. CHECK THE NET

http://www. filmwritten.org compares the film versions of the play by Franco Zeffirelli and Baz Lurhmann with *West Side Story*.

SCENE 3

- Friar Laurence agrees to arrange the secret marriage.
- The Friar, like the Prince, is anxious to end the feud between the two families.

Time: early Monday morning, immediately following II.2
(II.2.188–93; II.3.1–4, 28–30, 38)

Romeo visits Friar Laurence, who is glad to hear Romeo is no longer infatuated with Rosaline, but astonished to learn that another woman has taken her place. Nevertheless, he agrees to help arrange the marriage, as this may serve to unite the families of Montague and Capulet (note that this is the only justification for the Friar's willingness to assist in a secret marriage).

COMMENTARY

The Friar, like the Prince, Escalus, is anxious to end the feud. With the Church (the Friar) and the State (the Prince) both trying to heal old wounds, it is the more tragic that the love of Romeo and Juliet should be destroyed by this very quarrel and that only their deaths can bring about the reconciliation which the Friar here hopes their marriage will achieve.

The Friar's long opening **soliloquy** establishes him as kindly and good-natured and a man skilled in the poisons and medicines that may be made from plants. We are thus prepared to accept that he could make the potion he later gives to Juliet. More than this, the Friar's vision of the world as potentially good and evil underlines one of the main themes of the play: love and hate are very close, as poison and medicine may be derived from one plant, and should hate predominate, love will be destroyed. Some texts bring Romeo in at line 19, so that he overhears the last part of the speech: it is certainly true that the final lines of the speech are an unintentional prophecy of Romeo's fate, for he will die of poison because of the circumstances brought about by the hatred of Montagues and Capulets.

CHECK THE FILM

In Zeffirelli's film of *Romeo and Juliet* a glimpse of a crucifix prompts the Friar to think of the wedding as a means to heal the rift between the feuding families.

GLOSSARY

3	**osier cage** willow basket
4	**baleful** poisonous
10	**None but for some** there is no plant which does not have some good qualities
11	**mickle** great
12	**stones** rocks, in the sense of 'minerals'
14	**to the earth** that is, to the inhabitants of the earth
15	**strained** forced away, perverted
16	**Revolts ... abuse** turns away from its true nature if it is abused
21	**with that part** by means of that part (the nose, which smells the plant) revives ('cheers') the other parts of the body
25–6	**And where ... plant** the Friar here compares the spiritual state of man to the natural state of plants: as poison and medicine are found in one plant, so man has good and evil in him ('grace and rude will'); if the evil ('the worser') predominates, then the man is consumed by wickedness and spiritual death ('the canker death') overtakes him
27	**Benedicite** (Latin) 'May you be blessed'
29	**argues ... head** shows a disturbed mind
30	**good morrow** goodbye
33	**unbruised** unharmed by the world, that is, innocent
33	**unstuffed** not filled with troubles
36	**distemperature** uneasiness of mind
46–7	**one hath wounded ... wounded** that is, I fell in love with one who loves me; the wounds derive from Cupid's arrow. An apt image here as Juliet is Romeo's 'enemy'
49	**I ... hatred** that is, such as might be expected if one has been wounded by an enemy
50	**steads** helps
51	**homely** unsophisticated, that is, plain, straightforward
59	**pass** go along
65	**Jesu Maria** Jesus son of Mary
75	**sentence** saying, maxim

QUESTION

What is the importance of the feud to the scheme of the play?

> **GLOSSARY**
>
> 84 **Thy love ... spell** your expressions of love were as though recited ('read') by memory ('rote') by someone who could not understand ('spell') what he had learned to say: these comments point to the conventional and very ornate language Romeo has used to describe his feelings; unlike Juliet, who speaks plainly, as the Friar would wish, Romeo always uses the literary terms and images of Elizabethan love poetry
>
> 86 **In one respect** because of one thing
>
> 89 **stand on** insist on, or, depend on

Scene 4

- Tybalt has sent a challenge to Romeo.
- Preparations are made for the secret marriage.

Time: 12 noon on Monday (II.4.110)

Benvolio and Mercutio, who went home to bed at the end of II.1 without finding Romeo, are still looking for him the next morning. We hear from them that Tybalt has carried out his threat (I.5.91–2) not to ignore the matter of Romeo's intrusion into Capulet's party and has sent a challenge to Montague, which Benvolio believes Romeo will accept. When Romeo enters (coming from his meeting with the Friar) he is in good spirits (for the first time in the play) and engages in witty exchanges with Mercutio. In II.2.167–9 Juliet had arranged to send a messenger to Romeo, and now the Nurse comes. Romeo tells her to arrange for Juliet to go to confession that afternoon and says they will then be married by the Friar. He also arranges for his servant to give the Nurse a rope ladder, by means of which he will enter Juliet's room that night. The Nurse agrees to these plans.

> **CONTEXT**
>
> For a comic account of the stages by which a quarrel might escalate into a duel, see Touchstone's speech in Shakespeare's *As You Like It*, V.4.48-108.

COMMENTARY

Tybalt's behaviour is ominously at odds with the love that has developed in the previous scenes. Its introduction at this point, as Romeo and Juliet are preparing to escape from their families' hostility, creates a sense of unease which undercuts the exhilaration of Romeo's mood and the apparent progress of the lovers towards marriage. The happiness which they expect to result is already in jeopardy.

GLOSSARY

10	**answer** accept the challenge, though Mercutio jokingly takes it in its usual sense in the next line
11–12	**how he dares** saying that he dares to fight
13	**already dead** that is, through the sufferings of love
15	**pin** centre
16	**blind bow-boy's butt-shaft** Cupid's blunt arrow
19	**Prince of Cats** Tybalt's name was given to the cat in the old medieval story of Reynard the Fox
20–76	**He fights ... *hay*** Mercutio mocks Tybalt as a duellist skilled only with the slender, pointed Italian rapier, which pierces but does not cut the opponent; duels with such weapons only became fashionable in England in the 1590s, and were scorned by those, like Mercutio, who held that the heavier English sword, with its sharp edge to slash opponents, was the weapon for a real fight, requiring strength and valour
21	**as ... pricksong** as you sing carefully following printed music, that is, according to the rules
22	**rests ... rests** observes every detail of the music
23	**butcher ... button** because the rapier hits only a small point and does not cause a great wound like a sword
23–4	**duellist** the first use of the word in English literature; Mercutio uses it in scorn
24	**first house** finest school of duelling
25	**cause ... *hay*** these are all duelling terms
28	**The pox of** a plague on
28	**antic** grotesque
28–9	**affecting fantasticoes** affected fops
29	**new tuners** followers of every new fashion, who affect the latest idioms and forms of speech (Mercutio goes on to give examples)
33	**pardon-me** a new and over-used phrase among courtiers of the time (in Mercutio's view, a hypocritical phrase)
33–4	**who stand ... bench** Mercutio's usual wordplay: who insist ('stand') so much on the new code of manners ('form') that they cannot tolerate ('sit') the old ways ('bench')

 CHECK THE NET

For an introduction to Renaissance life and culture illustrating *Romeo and Juliet*, see **http://www.manteno.k12.il.us** and explore the High School Webquests link.

CONTEXT

The immensely popular work of the Italian poet Francesco Petrarch (1307–74) established styles of behaviour and of language which were to determine the conventions and discourse of love in the Renaissance.

GLOSSARY

37	**roe** several senses are combined: (i) the spawn of a fish, so 'unmanned'; (ii) a kind of deer, so 'without his dear one'; (iii) first syllable of Romeo's name, and so 'only half himself'
38	**numbers** verses
39	**Petrarch ... Laura** the famous medieval Italian poet Petrarch wrote of his love for Laura, and established many of those literary conventions and images which Elizabethan poets (and Romeo) still used
41–2	**Dido ... Thisbe** all famous women and lovers celebrated in Classical literature; that all their love affairs ended tragically strikes an ominous note
42	**hildings** worthless women
44	**slop** loose breeches (Romeo has not been to bed, and so has not changed since the party)
44–5	**gave ... counterfeit** deceived us
52	**bow in the hams** Mercutio takes 'courtesy' in line 50 as 'curtsey', and suggests Romeo spent the night bending his legs in lovemaking to Rosaline
53–85	**Meaning, to curtsey ... broad goose** now that he has arranged the marriage Romeo is in much better spirits and, for the first time in the play, is Mercutio's equal in wit: in these exchanges they play a number of word games: (i) courtesy, curtsey, courteous (lines 53–6); (ii) pink ('perfection', a flower and an ornament on a shoe, lines 56–9); (iii) pump (a shoe), sole (of a shoe), solely singular (uniquely remarkable), single-soled (weak), solely (only) and singleness (silliness, lines 59–65); (iv) wild goose-chase (a horse race in which all follow the leader, and so, a pointless chase), wild-goose (silly person), goose (prostitute and jester), cooked goose that needs sweetening (apple sauce) and broad goose (rude jester, lines 70–85)
68	**Swits** switch, riding crop or whip
82	**cheverel** kind of leather that stretches easily
83	**ell** measure of forty-five inches
89	**natural** idiot
90	**bauble** decorated stick, and a bawdy expression for penis
97	**occupy the argument** deal with the subject
98	**gear** matter
99	**A sail** Romeo means that he sees someone coming, as the look-out on a ship would cry 'a sail' when he sighted another ship

GLOSSARY

100	**shirt and a smock**	a man and a woman
110	**prick**	point, but the clock-hand is 'bawdy' because 'prick' also means 'penis'
110	**noon**	Juliet's go-between was supposed to arrive by 9 a.m. (II.2. 167–9), and Juliet had sent the Nurse on time (II.5.1); she has obviously been distracted from her purpose – that she should be late is entirely characteristic
115–16	**can … Romeo**	a rather strange question, since she had met Romeo the night before at the party (Act I.5.112–18, 134–6)
124	**confidence**	confidential, private conversation
126	**endite**	invite
127	**bawd**	woman who keeps a brothel; in what follows Mercutio is bawdy and rude, but not too mistaken about the Nurse's earthy nature
129	**hare**	slang for a prostitute
129	**lenten pie**	as no meat was supposed to be eaten during Lent, a hare pie would go stale
130	**hoar**	mouldy, and a pun on 'whore'
142	**merchant**	fellow (a term of derision)
143	**ropery**	bawdy jokes
145–6	**stand to**	maintain, carry out
149	**Jacks**	insolent fellows
150	**flirt-gills**	loose, immoral women
151	**skains-mates**	villainous companions
167	**weak**	contemptible
185	**tackled stair**	rope ladder
186	**topgallant**	summit
187	**convoy**	conveyance
188	**quit thy pains**	reward your efforts
193	**Two … away**	a proverb meaning that two can keep a secret, but not three
196	**prating**	chattering
197	**lay knife aboard**	a saying meaning 'to lay claim to'
201	**versal**	universal, whole
204	**dog's name**	because when pronounced 'R' sounds like a dog's growl (the Nurse is illiterate)
206	**sententious**	the Nurse (who quite often misuses words) means 'sentence', a saying
210	**apace**	quickly

CONTEXT

Romeo and Juliet is first mentioned by Francis Meres in his *Palladis Tamia*, an account of Elizabethan writers. Meres refers to the play as an example of how Shakespeare excels other writers in tragedy.

SCENE 5

- Juliet awaits the return of the nurse.
- She learns the arrangements for the marriage.

Time: early Monday afternoon, immediately following II.4 (II.4.110; II.5.1–11)

Juliet waits impatiently and anxiously for the return of the Nurse, who has been gone for three hours. When the Nurse does return, it is only after repeated questions that Juliet learns that Romeo has arranged the marriage for that afternoon.

COMMENTARY

This short scene achieves dramatic effect from the most unlikely material. The plot requires that Romeo's message is conveyed to Juliet, but, rather than a briefly uninteresting scene in which it is immediately delivered, the garrulousness of the Nurse builds the tension as the audience is made to wait, its impatience growing with Juliet's. The simple delivery of a message thus involves us in sympathy with Juliet, irritation and amusement at the Nurse, and relief when the plan is finally made known. That the scene ends with Juliet speaking of 'high fortune' (II. 5. 78) is ominous: in tragedy, it is when at the height of good fortune that the protagonist is mostly likely to fall.

CONTEXT

The marriage of Romeo and Juliet is depicted in Henry William Burnbury's watercolour, *Romeo and Juliet with Friar Laurence* (1794–6).

GLOSSARY	
3	**That's not so** That cannot be
7	**nimble-pinioned** swift-winged
7	**draw love** pull the chariot of the goddess of love, Venus
14	**bandy** strike a ball (see the previous line)
16	**feign ... dead** seem to be dead (because they move so slowly)
25	**leave** peace
26	**jaunce** jaunt, walk
36	**stay the circumstance** wait for the details
38	**simple** silly

GLOSSARY

62	**hot** impatient, passionate	
65	**coil** bother	
68	**hie** hurry	
74	**bird's nest** that is, Juliet's room	

SCENE 6

- Romeo and Juliet meet at the Friar's cell.
- The Friar promises to make short work of marrying them.

Time: later Monday afternoon (II.4.176–82; II.5.66–9)

In an unexpectedly quiet climax to the first movement of the play Romeo and Juliet meet at the Friar's cell and go in to be married.

COMMENTARY

By not presenting the marriage on stage, Shakespeare ensures that the memorable scenes will be the lovers' declaration of love (II.2) and their deaths (V.3). Thus, he gives a starkly simple design to the play. Our experience of it in the theatre is of sudden love and sudden death. The marriage seems, and is made by Shakespeare to seem, almost unimportant beside the love itself. The poetic and dramatic affirmation of love is the lover's exchange in II.2; the formal marriage is but a consequence of that.

By ending this movement of the play so quietly, Shakespeare achieves an obvious contrast with the violence that follows in the next scene: the idyllic, quiet, secret world of love is shattered by Tybalt. The Friar's opening words are cruelly **ironic** in view of what does happen later, and his words at lines 9–11 tragically prophetic.

? QUESTION
What bearing do the Friar's warnings about uncontrolled passion have on the concerns of the play?

GLOSSARY

3	**what sorrow can** whatever sorrows can	
15	**Too swift ... too slow** love that is too passionate ('Too swift') is as fallible as love that is too cold ('too slow')	

> **GLOSSARY**
>
> 17 **Will ... flint** Juliet walks so lightly her feet seem hardly to touch the ground and so will not wear out the rock ('flint')
>
> 18 **gossamers** cobwebs
>
> 19 **idles** drift
>
> 20 **vanity** the pleasures of the world; the Friar for a moment sadly remembers that, from the point of view of religion, such love is insubstantial
>
> 23 **As much ... much** Romeo's 'thanks' for Juliet's 'good evening' to the Friar (probably a kiss) will be too great a return for a single greeting and so she must include Romeo in it ('As much to him')
>
> 25 **and that** and since
>
> 29 **either** each other
>
> 30 **Conceit** imagination: the plain-speaking Juliet refuses Romeo's invitation to 'blazon' their love in fine phrases
>
> 34 **I ... wealth** I cannot add up ('sum') the total of half my wealth

ACT III

SCENE 1

- Mercutio dies at the hands of Tybalt.
- His death is avenged by Romeo who is then exiled from Verona.

Time: Monday afternoon, an hour after the marriage (III.1.112–3)

Mercutio and Benvolio are walking in Verona. Mercutio rejects Benvolio's suggestion that they should leave the streets as the Capulets are also out-of-doors and playfully mocks Benvolio's attempt to prevent any fighting by characterising him as extraordinarily quarrelsome. Mercutio is in fact describing his own character, for when they meet Tybalt Mercutio deliberately provokes him. Tybalt, however, is looking for Romeo, and, when he enters, Tybalt turns to him and insults him. We know that Tybalt is infuriated by Romeo's intrusion at Capulet's party but, to Romeo, newly married to Tybalt's cousin Juliet (and so now related to Tybalt himself), there seems to be no good reason to quarrel. Mercutio is dismayed by what he takes to be Romeo's cowardice in refusing to fight, and he himself draws his sword on Tybalt. As Romeo tries to stop them fighting, Mercutio is fatally wounded by Tybalt. In a moment of grim foresight, Romeo sees that this death will cause much sorrow in days to come, but, nevertheless, to avenge his friend's death, he fights and kills Tybalt. Benvolio persuades Romeo to flee, since the Prince has decreed that anyone guilty of further fighting will be punished by death (I.1.96–7). However, because Tybalt has himself committed a murder, the Prince does not order Romeo's execution, but exiles him from Verona.

CONTEXT

The late seventeenth century poet, John Dryden, reported Shakespeare as saying that he 'was obliged to kill Mercutio in the third Act' lest he came to dominate the play.

COMMENTARY

Thus, in the scene immediately following the marriage, the event which will part the lovers occurs. It is the pivotal scene of the play, on which the fortune of the protagonists turns. Throughout the second act the lovers' fortunes have been steadily improving: Romeo and Juliet exchanged vows in II.2; in II.3 the Friar agreed to marry them; in II.4 Romeo was in high spirits and told the Nurse of his plan; and in II.6 the marriage was accomplished. Now, in a moment, the movement towards tragedy (of which we had hints in I.4.106–111; I.5.91–2; II.4.6–9, and for which the Chorus has prepared us) begins. It is sadly **ironic** that Romeo himself does his best to prevent it: it is the misguided sense of honour of his friend, Mercutio, which brings it about.

GLOSSARY		
2	**Capels**	Capulets
8	**operation**	effect
9	**drawer**	waiter
11	**hot**	impetuous
15	**two**	Mercutio's wordplay on Benvolio's 'to' in line 14
23	**addle as an egg**	bad as a rotten egg
31	**fee simple**	full title

CHECK THE BOOK

On fighting in the play, see Charles Edelman, *Brawl Ridiculous: Swordfighting in Shakespeare's Plays*, 1972.

GLOSSARY

31–2	**for an hour … quarter** before an hour and a quarter had passed; Benvolio means that were he as quarrelsome as Mercutio he would be killed in a fight within this time; it is dramatically **ironic** that Mercutio will be killed within this time because of his quarrelsomeness
45	**Consort … minstrels** Tybalt in line 44 meant 'associate with' by **'consortest'**, but a company of musicians was called a 'consort' and Mercutio sees this as an opportunity to take offence since 'minstrel' (a hired musician) was a term of abuse
47	**fiddlestick** i.e., his sword
56	**livery** Mercutio, still looking for grievances, takes 'man' in line 55 as 'servant' and exclaims that Romeo does not wear the uniform ('livery') of one of Tybalt's hired men
58	**worship** honour; a polite form of address here used ironically by Mercutio, who means that Romeo is Tybalt's servant, or follower, only in the sense that he will follow him to the place for a duel ('field')
62	**excuse … rage** excuse me from showing the appropriate rage
68	**devise** guess
70	**tender** value
73	*Alla stoccata* a duelling term which Mercutio sarcastically uses as a name for Tybalt
77–8	**as … me** depending on how you treat me
78	**dry-beat** cudgel, beat without drawing blood
79	**pilcher** scabbard
87	**bandying** fighting
91	**sped** slain
94	**villain** a term of address to a servant, not here implying bad qualities, as it does in Tybalt's use to the gentleman Romeo in line 60, to which Romeo refers in line 125
98	**grave man** a serious man and a man in a grave; an appropriate, and moving, jest from the dying Mercutio, who has not once been serious in the play
98–9	**peppered** killed
102	**book of arithmetic** book of rules
107	**worms' meat** i.e., a corpse
109	**ally** relative
113	**cousin** relative, through his marriage to Juliet

GLOSSARY

114 **effeminate** like a woman, i.e., unmanly (the distinction between robust manhood and soft womanhood was conventional)

115 **temper** character

117 **aspired** risen to

119 **on more ... depend** portends ill fortune on more days to come: this, and the following line, marked out as a **couplet**, signal the beginning of the tragedy

123 **respective lenity** leniency or mildness which is respectful (to Tybalt, as Juliet's, and now, Romeo's, relative)

124 **conduct** conductor, guide

131 **This** i.e., Romeo's sword

133 **up** aroused

134 **amazed** bewildered, dazed (a stronger word in Elizabethan English than it is now)

142 **discover** reveal

143 **unlucky manage** unfortunate handling

148 **true** faithful to your word

154 **nice** petty, trivial

154–5 **urged ... displeasure** that is, tried to dissuade Tybalt from fighting by reminding him of the Prince's decree against feuding: Benvolio biases his account in Romeo's favour for, although Romeo did 'speak Tybalt fair', he had not mentioned the Prince's displeasure; there is thus some truth in Lady Capulet's later remark, lines 176–7

157 **unruly spleen** ungovernable bad temper

158 **but that** so that

164 **Retorts** returns

168 **envious** hostile

171 **newly entertained** only just thought of

185 **His fault ... end** in killing Tybalt Romeo had only anticipated the law, which would have condemned Tybalt to death for murdering Mercutio

189 **My blood** the blood of my family (as Mercutio was his relative)

190 **amerce** punish by a fine

191 **mine** my relative

193 **purchase out** buy off, obliterate

196 **attend our will** take heed of what I command

197 **Mercy ... kill** if the law is merciful to murderers then it simply encourages further murders

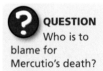

QUESTION
Who is to blame for Mercutio's death?

SCENE 2

- News of Tybalt's death and Romeo's banishment is brought to Juliet.
- The Nurse agrees to bring Romeo to Juliet.

Time: later Monday afternoon, three hours after the marriage (III.2.99) *and two hours after Romeo's fight* (III.1.112–13)

Juliet is waiting impatiently for the night, which will bring Romeo to her (as he had planned before their marriage II.4.183–7; II.5.72–4). In a strikingly dramatic moment, just as Juliet is taken up with joyful thoughts of Romeo and the consummation of their love, the Nurse enters to dash all her hopes by telling her of Tybalt's death and Romeo's banishment. (A very similar technique is used by Shakespeare at the beginning of V.1.) To the Nurse's surprise, after a moment's shock at what Romeo has done, Juliet is not appalled that he has killed her cousin Tybalt, but full of grief at his banishment. The scene ends with the Nurse agreeing to bring Romeo from Friar Laurence's cell, where he has hidden since the fight.

COMMENTARY

This is a scene of **tragic irony**. As it opens, the audience, which already knows of Tybalt's death, is aware that what is, in effect, Juliet's wedding hymn will lead to no such happiness as she anticipates. When Juliet herself comes to realise that the wedding night is now to be the lovers' farewell, she speaks **metaphorically** of this parting as her death, darkening the atmosphere of the play and, unknowingly, alerting the audience to her fate. Juliet's vulnerability is underscored by the audience's prior knowledge of what has occurred, and its realisation of what will occur.

CHECK THE NET
Look on the Net for John R.S. Stanhope's oil painting of *Juliet and her Nurse* (1863), which was much praised for the richness of its colours and its Pre-Raphaelite medievalism.

GLOSSARY

1–2	**Gallop … Phoebus' lodging** Juliet is referring to the horses pulling the sun god's chariot across the sky, i.e., she wants sunset to arrive quickly

GLOSSARY

3	**Phaëton** Phoebus allowed his son Phaëton to drive his chariot, who was unable to prevent it racing too near the earth and was destroyed by a thunderbolt from Zeus lest the world be consumed by fire
5	**close** enclosing, concealing
6	**runaway's** a famous crux (that is, a textual passage which puzzles commentators): who it is that is a 'runaway' is not clear, but the general sense is that the lovers will be safe in the darkness, free from spies
10	**civil** decorous, gentle
12	**lose … match** Juliet must yield her body to Romeo ('lose') and so win a husband
14	**Hood … blood** Juliet is asking the night to hide ('hood') her blushes ('blood') as she yields her virginity, but the image, from falconry, is appropriate in other ways: the head of an untrained ('unmanned') falcon was covered with a hood until it grew used to its owner (or 'man'); Juliet is untrained in the ways of love-making and 'unmanned' because she has not yet had a man as a lover
14	**bating** fluttering
35	**cords** ropes (that Romeo had given her, II.4.183–7)
37	**weraday** alas
38	**undone** ruined
40	**envious** full of hostility, malicious
40	**Romeo can** the Nurse means that Romeo can be so full of hostility as to kill Tybalt
49	**Or those … 'Ay'** if you must answer 'yes' because those eyes (that is, Romeo's) are shut (that is, he is dead)
53	**God save the mark** a common Elizabethan exclamation when something awful or disagreeable was mentioned
54	**corse** corpse
56	**swounded** swooned
59	**Vile earth** that is, her own body
60	**heavy** literally, and meaning 'sad'
64	**so contrary** in such opposite directions (Juliet thought the Nurse had been describing Romeo's body)
67	**dreadful trumpet** in Christian belief the Day of Judgement (Doomsday) will be announced by the sound of a trumpet

CONTEXT

In 1750, 'The Romeo and Juliet War' saw rival productions running at the Drury Lane and Covent Garden theatres in London.

CHECK THE BOOK

On the power of sexual desire in the play, see Michael Goldman, *Shakespeare and the Energies of Drama*, 1972.

GLOSSARY

73	**serpent** when the Devil tempted Eve in Paradise he appeared as a snake ('serpent'): Juliet is, for a moment, appalled that her lover could have done such a thing, and throughout this speech compares his apparently deceptive mildness with the deceptive appearance of the 'fiend' Satan; but when the Nurse agrees that men are all deceivers, Juliet quickly recovers her faith in Romeo
81	**bower** enclose, embower
87	**naught** wicked
117	**And needly … ranked** must be accompanied
120	**modern** ordinary
126	**sound** express
139	**wot** know

SCENE 3

- The Friar advises the despairing Romeo to flee to Mantua while he seeks to reconcile the feuding families and to gain a pardon from the Prince.

- Romeo contemplates suicide but is warned against it by the Friar.

Time: late on Monday evening (III.3.164, 172)

Since killing Tybalt Romeo has hidden in Friar Laurence's cell (III.2.141). The Friar now tells him that he is banished by the Prince which, as it means separation from Juliet, is to Romeo only another way of condemning him to death. The Nurse comes, as she had promised Juliet she would (III.2.140–1), and her description of Juliet's grief so fills Romeo with guilt and regret that he tries to kill himself. Horrified at this, the Friar in a long speech shows Romeo the folly of suicide; tells him that he has much to be thankful for; urges him to go that night to Juliet, as arranged (II.4.183–7; II.5.72–4), to comfort her; and then to leave Verona for Mantua, where he may live until such time as the Friar can publicly proclaim the marriage, reconcile the families and gain a pardon from the Prince. To all this, Romeo agrees. The Nurse leaves to tell Juliet that

Romeo is coming, and the scene ends with the Friar warning Romeo to leave Verona with care, and assuring him that he will keep in touch with him through Romeo's servant (Balthasar).

COMMENTARY

This scene balances III.2: that had presented Juliet's reaction to the news of Tybalt's death and Romeo's banishment; we now see how Romeo responds to his bad fortune. The Nurse herself parallels them in III.3.85–6.

CHECK THE NET

For information on *West Side Story*, the musical film version of *Romeo and Juliet*, visit **http://www.filmsite .org/wests.html**.

GLOSSARY		
2	**parts**	personal qualities
10	**vanished from**	escaped from (and so vanished into air)
17	**without**	outside, beyond
44	**deadly sin**	the Friar exclaims at what seems to him to be the sin of ingratitude for what is, legally, mercy, since the Prince could have had Romeo put to death
45	**Thy fault … death**	our law prescribes death for thy fault
46	**rushed**	a strange word, perhaps a printer's error for 'brushed' or 'thrust'
33	**validity**	value
39	**Still blush**	Romeo supposes Juliet's innocence such that her lips will blush for 'kissing' each other when they touch
46	**mean … mean**	means … however distasteful
52	**mangle**	mutilate, torture
53	**fond**	foolish
60	**Displant**	move
61	**prevails not**	cannot prevail in argument, convince
64	**dispute … estate**	discuss the state of your affairs
78	**simpleness**	folly; Romeo's folly is that he remains lying on the ground (line 70) and will not hide
86	**woeful sympathy**	Romeo 'sympathises', or identifies, with Juliet in that he behaves exactly like her in his grief (or 'woe')
91	**O**	the sound of moaning
103	**level**	aim
107	**sack**	plunder
113	**ill-beseeming**	inappropriate, unnatural
115	**tempered**	formed, balanced
122	**wit**	intellectual ability

CONTEXT

There is no record of an Elizabethan performance of *Romeo and Juliet*, but when first published in 1597 its title page stated that it had been 'often plaid publiquely'.

GLOSSARY

127	**Digressing**	if it deviates
129	**Killing**	if it kills
132	**flask**	container for gunpowder
136	**dead**	wishing to be dead
143	**mishavèd**	misbehaved
148	**Watch be set**	at nightfall the city gates would be closed and a guard ('Watch') set
151	**blaze**	proclaim
165	**comfort**	cheerfulness
171	**hap**	happening
171	**chances**	occurs
174	**brief**	with so brief a farewell, that is, hurriedly

SCENE 4

- Lord Capulet arranges a marriage between Juliet and Paris.
- His wife is to tell Juliet.

Time: night-time, very early Tuesday morning (III.4.5–7, 34–5)

The lovers have not been seen together since the short scene of their marriage (II.6). Since then, in III.2 and III.3 we have seen their separate reactions to the ill-fortune which has intervened, but, before they come together to take their farewell (in what will prove to be their last scene together until their deaths) Shakespeare keeps the audience in anticipation by turning aside for a moment to introduce a new complication, a stroke of fate which is to hasten the tragedy. He had prepared for this in I.2–3 when we learned of Paris's suit for Juliet. Then Capulet had said that he would follow Juliet's wishes in the matter (I.2.16–19), but, now that Tybalt's death has so disturbed the family that he has not been able to discuss it with her, he tells Paris that he is sure Juliet will obey her father and so he goes ahead to arrange the marriage for Thursday without consulting Juliet. His wife, Lady Capulet, is to tell her (not ask her).

COMMENTARY

There is **dramatic irony** and **tragic irony** in this scene. In view of Juliet's obedience and compliance in I.3 it is no wonder that Capulet is so confident she will obey him now. He is, of course, proved wrong, and the staging of the scene at this moment in the plot underlines this in a dramatically ironic way. There is a contrast implied between this marriage arranged by parents and the marriage, resulting from love, which is about to be consummated in Juliet's room. Juliet has now moved far from I.3; her parents act as though she is still the same girl, but she is now, unknown to them (but not to the audience), a married woman awaiting her bridegroom. At the same time, unknown to the lovers, events are working against their relationship and threatening their love (tragic irony). The audience is in the privileged position of understanding more about Juliet than her parents, and of knowing more about her parents' plans than Juliet.

GLOSSARY

2	**move** persuade
6	**promise** assure
11	**mewed ... heaviness** shut up with her grief; Juliet's real cause of grief is, of course, not Tybalt's death, as her mother supposes, but Romeo's banishment, and she is shut up in her room only for Romeo to come to her
12	**desperate tender** bold offer
23	**keep no great ado** not have an elaborate ceremony with many guests
24	**late** recently
25	**held him carelessly** did not esteem ('held') him dearly
31	**ere you go to bed** this introduces a moment's suspense: it was late at night that Romeo left the Friar (III.3.172), and if Lady Capulet goes now to Juliet's room she will either find Romeo there or be there when he arrives; Lady Capulet does, in fact, disturb the lovers (III.5.39–40)
32	**against** for

SCENE 5

- After spending the night together, Romeo and Juliet part.
- Juliet refuses to marry Paris.

Time: dawn on Tuesday (III.5.1–2, 6–10, 40)

In this, only the fourth scene in which they have been together (I.5, II.2, II.6), the lovers have to admit that day is dawning and, unless they part, Romeo will be captured and put to death for not going into exile (as the Prince had decreed, III.1.194–5). The Nurse interrupts them to say that Juliet's mother is coming (as she had been told to do by Capulet, III.4.15, 31), and so Romeo leaves. Juliet, filled with misgivings, fears that they will never meet again. Just as Juliet has bid her husband farewell, she is told by her mother that in two days she must marry Paris. Lady Capulet says that Juliet's father has arranged this so as to stop her grieving for Tybalt. He wants her to have an occasion for joy. Paris himself gives the same explanation in the next scene (IV.1.9–15), and this would explain why Capulet went ahead in III.4 without consulting Juliet.

Juliet flatly refuses the marriage and, when her father comes in, he is furious at this disobedience, shocking both the Nurse and Lady Capulet by the violence of his anger and the insults he hurls at Juliet. He swears that unless Juliet obeys him he will never see her again. In comic contrast, the Nurse happily suggests that Juliet should indeed marry Paris as Romeo is unlikely ever to be able to return. Juliet is naturally appalled at this, and, as Romeo had sought out the Friar when he wished to marry Juliet (II.3) and after killing Tybalt (III.3), so, in this new difficulty, Juliet decides to go to him for help.

COMMENTARY

The play does not depict Romeo's arrival at Juliet's room, only his departure. It is another way in which the atmosphere is darkened: sorrowful parting, rather than joyous greeting, sets the mood. Juliet's fears that she will never again see Romeo similarly strengthen the impression that the tragedy is now gathering

CHECK THE NET
Search the Net to see if you can find the poet and engraver, William Blake's colour print *The Dance of Albion* (c. 1794) which is thought to have been inspired by Romeo's leaving at dawn.

momentum, as does Romeo's remark in line 36 that the lovers' predicament darkens the lighter the day becomes. As their parting occurs at dawn, some time has passed since Romeo left the Friar late on Monday night (III.3.172). The assumption is that during the night Romeo has been with Juliet and consummated their marriage. Indeed, it adds to the **irony** of III.4 if Romeo is actually with Juliet as her father is arranging her marriage to Paris. This would mean that the secret love match is being consummated (and so confirmed emotionally and legally) even as Capulet plans a public wedding for Juliet. That plan is another example of **tragic irony**: hoping to make Juliet happy Capulet in fact achieves the exact opposite and contributes to those circumstances which bring about her death.

CONTEXT

In a poem prefixed to the First Folio edition of Shakespeare's plays (1623), Shakespeare's friend and rival dramatist Ben Jonson saluted him as 'the wonder of our Stage' and 'not of an age, but of all time!'

GLOSSARY	
3	**fearful** frightened
7	**envious** malicious
13	**exhales** draws up; meteors were thought to be drawn up from the earth, ignited and 'exhaled' by the sun
18	**so** if
20	**reflex of Cynthia's brow** reflection of the moon (Cynthia was goddess of the moon)
23	**care** desire, concern
28	**sharps** musical notes
29	**division** music; Juliet puns on the word in the next line
31	**Some … change eyes** the toad, having more beautiful eyes than the lark, was said to have exchanged his eyes for those of the more attractive lark
34	**hunt's up** early morning song to wake huntsmen; as newly married couples were similarly awakened, the term was used in this context too
46	**be much in years** have aged many years
54	**ill-divining soul** soul which foresees bad fortune
67	**procures** brings
74	**feeling** deeply felt: Juliet's mother believes Juliet means the death of Tybalt when in fact she suffers for the loss of Romeo
75	**friend** to Lady Capulet this means Tybalt; to the audience, Romeo
81	**asunder** apart
86	**venge** avenge

QUESTION
In what ways does the ferocity of Capulet's anger with his daughter offer an insight into the sexual politics of the play?

GLOSSARY	
88	**Mantua** Lady Capulet cannot possibly know this: Romeo, who has only this moment left the room, can hardly yet be in Mantua, and, anyway, only the Friar and (presumably) Juliet know of his plan
89	**runagate** renegade
90	**dram** small drink; Lady Capulet means poison; ironically, it will be Romeo who poisons himself
94	**dead** Juliet is deliberately ambiguous: to her mother she says she wants Romeo dead; her true meaning is that her heart is dead as Romeo has left
97	**temper** her mother takes Juliet to mean 'mix'; we take the meaning 'moderate' or 'weaken'
101	**wreak** avenge
107	**careful** considerate
109	**sorted out** arranged
109	**sudden** unexpected
111	**in happy time** opportunely (ironically said)
119	**he that should be** he that wants to be
125	**at your hands** from you
127	**brother's** brother-in-law's (see III.1.146)
129	**conduit** water pipe (Juliet is crying)
131	**bark** boat
136	**overset** overturn
139	**will none** will have none of it
141	**Take me with you** let me understand you
143	**proud** grateful, pleased
145	**bride** bridegroom
148	**But thankful ... love** but, though I hate what you have arranged, I am grateful to you who intended I should love it
149	**chopped logic** hair splitting, quibbling with words
151	**minion** worthless girl
153	**fettle** groom a horse, that is, get ready, prepare
153	**joints** limbs, that is, her body, herself
155	**hurdle** sledge on which criminals were dragged to their punishment
156	**green-sickness carrion** pallid as a corpse
156	**baggage** hussy, good-for-nothing
157	**tallow** hard, yellowy fat from which candles were made

GLOSSARY

160	**Hang thee** may you be hanged
164	**My fingers itch** that is, I itch to strike her
165	**lent** given; in Christian thought all things on earth are but lent during life
168	**hilding** worthless girl
169	**rate** berate, scold
171	**Prudence** probably not the Nurse's real Christian name, but used sarcastically by Capulet
171	**Smatter … gossips** chatter with your friends, and not with me
172	**God … e'en** in bidding her good evening Capulet is telling the Nurse to go
174	**gravity** wisdom (Capulet is being ironic)
176	**God's bread** the bread blessed in the Holy Communion service
179	**matched** married
181	**demesnes** estates, lands
184	**puling** whining, whimpering
185	**mammet** puppet
185	**in her fortune's tender** when fortune makes her an offer
188	**an** if
189	**Graze** feed: Capulet insults Juliet by using a word applied to animals
190	**do not use** am not accustomed
191	**Advise** consider
195	**Nor what … good** nor shall anything of mine ever help you
196	**be forsworn** break my word
203	**a word** that is, a word to your father on your behalf
207	**faith** vow, that is, her marriage vow
210	**practise stratagems** use cunning schemes
214	**all the world to nothing** it is a safe bet
215	**challenge** claim
220	**dishclout** dishcloth
222	**Beshrew … heart** curse me if I'm wrong
236	**Ancient damnation** damned old woman
239	**compare** comparison
241	**twain** two, that is, separated

CONTEXT

The late seventeenth-century poet John Dryden believed Shakespeare 'was the man who of all Modern, and perhaps Ancient Poets, had the largest and most comprehensive soul'.

ACT IV

SCENE 1

- Juliet and Paris meet at the Friar's cell.
- The Friar plans to fake Juliet's death.

Time: Tuesday (IV.1.90), and, as both Paris and Juliet have come straight to the Friar following conversations at dawn on Tuesday, the morning of that day

In this scene Juliet and her suitor, Paris, meet for the only time in the play. Paris has come to see the Friar to tell him of his planned marriage with Juliet. He explains that the haste is because Capulet wants to lessen his daughter's grief at Tybalt's death. Juliet enters (she had resolved to visit the Friar at the end of III.5), and carefully avoids answering directly Paris's questions about her love for him and their marriage. Paris leaves, thinking Juliet is to confess to the Friar. In fact, she implores his help in avoiding the marriage with Paris. The Friar suggests that the night before her wedding (that is, tomorrow, Wednesday, night) she should take a potion he can give her which will make her appear to be dead but from the effects of which she will awake unharmed, as from a sleep. When she is found on her wedding day, all will think her dead, and she will be placed in the Capulet vault. The Friar, meanwhile, will inform Romeo of the plan by letter, and he and Romeo will be there when Juliet awakes. Romeo can then take her back to Mantua with him. To this desperate plan Juliet agrees.

QUESTION
How believable is the character of the Friar and how credible his schemes?

COMMENTARY

As in III.5 where Juliet and Lady Capulet had spoken at cross purposes, so, now, there are two meanings in the exchange between Juliet and Paris.

GLOSSARY		
3	**And I am ... haste**	no reluctance of mine will lessen his haste
5	**Uneven**	irregular, contrary to normal practice
9	**counts**	accounts, considers

GLOSSARY

13	**minded … alone** remembered or dwelt upon when she is alone
29	**abused** spoilt, marred
31	**For it was** for my face was
34	**to my face** directly, and, about my face
36	**not mine own** because, although Paris does not know this, it is Romeo's
40	**entreat … alone** ask you to leave us alone at this time
41	**shield** forbid
47	**compass** limit
48	**prorogue** delay, postpone
54	**presently** immediately
57	**label** seal, that is, confirm another marriage by holding another hand
57	**deed** legal document, that is, a binding marriage certificate
59	**this shall slay** this knife shall slay
62	**extremes** desperate situation
64	**commission** authority
68	**Hold** wait
74	**chide away … shame** drive away this disgrace
75	**copest with** encounters
75	**'scape from it** that is, escape from shame
81	**charnel house** small building next to a church in which were placed bones disturbed when new graves were dug
83	**reeky shanks** damp and stinking shin-bones
83	**chapless** jawless
88	**unstained** faithful, not stained with infidelity
93	**vial** small bottle
94	**distilling liquor** drink which will spread through the body
96	**humour** feeling
97	**native progress** natural movement
97	**surcease** stop
100	**wanny** wan, pale
102	**supple government** ability to move
103	**against … awake** in preparation for your awakening
119	**inconstant toy** whim
122	**prosperous** successful

CONTEXT

Early commentators thought Shakespeare's achievement extraordinary when he had no social advantages and had not been to university. That 'his learning was very little' (Thomas Fuller) led to the idea that he was an untutored 'natural' genius.

SCENE 2

- Following the Friar's plan, Juliet agrees to marry Paris.
- The wedding is brought forward by a day.

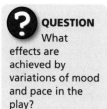

QUESTION What effects are achieved by variations of mood and pace in the play?

Time: 'near night' on Tuesday (IV.2.39)

In the Capulet house preparations are going forward for the wedding. Juliet, falling in with the Friar's plan, submits entirely to her father, who is so pleased that he brings forward the wedding to the next day, Wednesday. Since the change of day will mean still less time for preparation, Capulet will himself stay up all night to help to get things ready in time. The scene ends on an ironic note: Capulet's heart is 'wondrous light' (line 46) now that Juliet has agreed to marry Paris: the audience knows she has quite other intentions.

COMMENTARY

Act IV Scene 1 could only have taken place on Tuesday morning as both Paris and Juliet visit the Friar directly after their conversation in III.4 and III.5 at dawn on Tuesday. In this scene Juliet returns straight from that visit, so it cannot yet be, as Lady Capulet says, 'late' on Tuesday. The time-scale is shortened for dramatic effect so that we come quickly to the crucial Tuesday night.

It is a cruel irony that Juliet's pretended change of heart is thus so effective that it contributes to the tragedy, for that lost day will help prevent Romeo learning the truth about the Friar's plan.

GLOSSARY	
2	**cunning** skilful
3	**try** test
4	**can lick their fingers** proverbially the mark of a good cook
10	**unfurnished** unprepared in not having the necessary food ready
14	**harlotry** waywardness
16	**gadding** wandering
19	**behests** commands

GLOSSARY

20	**enjoined** directed
26	**becomèd** proper
33	**closet** private room
39	**stir about** busy myself

SCENE 3

- Juliet sends away the Nurse.
- She takes the Friar's potion.

Time: Tuesday night (IV.3.12–3)

Juliet sends away the Nurse (as the Friar had directed, IV.1.92) and takes the potion.

As the marriage is now on Wednesday, not Thursday, she is taking it a day earlier than the Friar had planned (IV.1.89–94).

COMMENTARY

Juliet's **soliloquy**, dwelling on her fear of the vault, enlarges what she had already said to the Friar (IV.1.80–8) and darkens the atmosphere of death which is gathering in the play. By referring us yet again to the Capulet vault, the speech reinforces the fear that in some way it is connected with the tragic climax of the play.

CONTEXT

In Shakespeare's day, wild and garden plants played a very large role in medicine, and could be easily culled from the hedgerows. Many were known to have somniferous properties. Gerard's *Herbal*, written in 1597, lists some twenty sleep-inducing plants, including the opium poppy, which he says 'provoke[s] sleepe' and 'somewhat too plentifully taken doth also bring death'.

GLOSSARY

1	**attires** clothes
5	**cross** perverse
7	**culled** selected
8	**behoveful** needed
8	**state** ceremony
25	**ministered** provided
29	**tried** proved
35	**strangled** suffocated
36	**like** likely

? QUESTION
What is the effect of intercutting the story of Romeo and Juliet with scenes reminding the audience of everyday life and conventional expectations?

GLOSSARY

37	**conceit**	imagining
49	**distraught**	mad
50	**Environèd**	surrounded
53	**rage**	madness
56	**spit**	pierce through, impale

SCENE 4

- Lord Capulet prepares for the wedding of Juliet and Paris.
- There is much excitement.

Time: 3 a.m. on Wednesday (IV.4.3–4)

Capulet has been up all night helping to prepare the wedding feast. These preparations generate excitement and fun, with Capulet good-naturedly joking with the servants and ordering them about, hurrying everyone as much as he can.

COMMENTARY

This short scene gives the impression of time passing: it fills in the night while Juliet is drugged, for, at the end of the scene, we are told that the bridegroom, Paris, has arrived. Thus, it bridges Tuesday night (IV.3) and Wednesday morning (IV.5). More important, however, is its dramatically effective change of mood. Its happy and boisterous confusion is in studied contrast to the sombre quiet of Juliet's soliloquy in IV.3 and the outbursts of grief which are to follow in IV.5. The contrast sharpens our awareness that, apart from this noisy preparation and excited anticipation of the wedding, alone in her room, Juliet has taken the potion which will bring all this furious activity to nothing. In much the same way, Capulet's plans to marry Juliet to Paris in III.4 had been rendered **ironic** by our knowledge that, even as he spoke, Juliet was either with, or waiting for, Romeo in her room. In each case the audience has a fuller knowledge of the situation than have the characters on the stage and, because of this, it knows that what the characters are doing will come to nothing. In III.4 it knew, and Capulet did not, that Juliet was already married; here, it knows, and Capulet does not, that Juliet will go to the vault as if dead and not to her wedding with Paris.

CONTEXT

For another example of a heroine seemingly dead after taking a potion, see Shakespeare's *Cymbeline*.

GLOSSARY

2	**pastry** part of the kitchen
4	**curfew bell** bell that tolls the hour
6	**cot-quean** man who does woman's work (as Capulet had promised he would, IV.2.43)
8	**watching** staying awake, lack of sleep
9	**whit** bit
11	**mouse hunt** up at night after a woman ('mouse')
12	**watch ... watching now** watch you to make sure you don't go off at night like that now
13	**jealous hood** jealous woman
18	**have a head that will** have brains enough to
20	**Mass** a common exclamation, from 'By the Mass'
20	**whoreson** rascally fellow
21	**loggerhead** blockhead, a pun on 'logs' in lines 16 and 18
21	**Good Father** an exclamation, perhaps a misprint for the common 'Good Faith'
25	**trim** dress

SCENE 5

- Juliet is discovered apparently dead.
- The Friar takes over proceedings.

Time: early Wednesday morning, straight after IV.5 (IV.4.25–8; IV.5.1)

The Nurse (who for the first time is not in Juliet's confidence) goes to wake Juliet and finds her apparently dead. The Friar arrives and, amidst the family's exclamations of grief, takes charge to ensure that Juliet is carried to the family vault as he had planned.

CONTEXT

No one knows whether the famous portrait of a bald Shakespeare wearing a ruff, engraved by Martin Droeshout for the 1623 First Folio edition of the plays, is in fact a good likeness.

COMMENTARY

The scene is constructed to inhibit the audience from sharing the sorrow of the household, for the real cause of grief is yet to come with the true death of Juliet. The exaggerated language of the laments of the Nurse, Paris and Capulet, which almost become ridiculous; the Friar's speeches, which remind the audience that this is all part of a plan; and the comedy of the musicians with which the scene ends, all prevent the audience's sympathies from being too deeply aroused.

GLOSSARY

1	**Fast**	fast asleep
4	**pennyworths**	allowances of sleep
6	**set up his rest**	to stake all one's money at the card game of primero, and so the meaning here is 'is determined'; the Nurse means that Paris will keep Juliet awake the next night by making love to her
26	**settled**	congealed
37	**deflowerèd by him**	lost her virginity to him (that is, death)
45	**lasting**	endless, everlasting
55	**spited**	treated spitefully
60	**Uncomfortable**	depriving us of our comfort
65	**Confusion**	calamity, disaster
66	**confusions**	disorders
69	**Your part**	that is, her body
70	**his part**	that is, her soul
83	**Yet … merriment**	reason, which knows there is no real cause for grief, laughs at the tears which natural affection makes us shed
96	**put … pipes**	pack up our instruments
98	**case**	situation
99	**case**	container for a musical instrument
100	**'Heart's ease'**	a popular song of the time
103–4	**'My heart is full'**	another song
104	**dump**	a dismal tune (Peter is muddling his terms)
110	**give it you soundly**	play it loudly and pay you back for refusing
112	**gleek**	mockery, scorn
112–13	**give you the minstrel**	call you a good-for-nothing

GLOSSARY

114–15	**serving-creature** like 'minstrel' a term of derision
116	**pate** head
116	**carry no crotchets** tolerate none of your whims; literally, 'crotchets' are musical notes
116	**re … fa** musical notes
117	**note** understand or pay attention, a pun on 'note' meaning 'set to music'
121	**put out** display
125	**'When griping … silver sound'** the beginning of a published poem in praise of music
125	**griping** agonising
126	**dumps** depression
127	**Catling** a lute string, and so a humorous surname for a musician
132	**Rebeck** a fiddle
135	**Soundpost** part of a violin
138	**cry you mercy** beg your pardon
139	**for sounding** for making music

? QUESTION
What is the significance of the many musical allusions and references in the play?

ACT V

SCENE 1

- Romeo's servant arrives in Mantua with the mistaken news of Juliet's death.
- Romeo buys poison to kill himself in the vault where she lies.

Time: later on Wednesday

The Friar's plan of feigning Juliet's death, successfully carried out in IV.5, was intended to solve the lovers' problems. In this, the very next scene, we learn that Fate is not to be so easily thwarted. Romeo, who left Juliet early on Tuesday morning in II.5, is now in Mantua. As the scene opens, he is confidently expecting good news

CONTEXT

'I defy you stars':
Edmund in
Shakespeare's *King
Lear* mocks the
belief that stars
control human
destinies, but
astrology, which
holds that the
influence of
celestial bodies
affects human
lives,was a strong
current in the
thinking of the
Renaissance. It is
alluded to in the
description in the
Prologue of
Romeo and Juliet
as 'star-crossed'
lovers.

from Verona. These hopes are dashed immediately his servant, Balthasar, arrives to tell him Juliet is dead. Although the Friar had arranged to send news to Romeo in his exile through Friar John (III.3.169–71), Romeo has heard nothing. Nor does Balthasar have any letters from the Friar for Romeo and clearly does not know the truth about Juliet's 'death'. Romeo resolves to return to Verona that night, to poison himself at the vault where Juliet lies. He buys a poison for his purpose from an apothecary in Mantua.

COMMENTARY

It is not clear from the scene itself on which day it occurs. We do know that the last scene of the play is set during the night that follows the day of this scene. Romeo is here in Mantua, and says that he will be back in Verona to lie with Juliet 'tonight' (V.1.26, 34), and in V.3 we see him arrive at the vault. But is this scene set on Wednesday, the day of Juliet's entombment (IV.5), or on Thursday? In other words, does Romeo kill himself on the night following Juliet's supposed 'death' or twenty-four hours later?

On the one hand, the Friar had said that Juliet would be drugged for forty-two hours (IV.1.105). As she took the potion on Tuesday night (IV.3), she would wake up on Thursday night. For Romeo to be there when she wakes in V.3 his 'tonight' should mean Thursday night, which would place this scene on Thursday. Later in the play, just after Juliet has woken, the Watch says she has been in the vault for two days (V.3.176), so V.3, set when it is dark, just before dawn, seems to occur very early on Friday (so that Juliet has been in the tomb on Wednesday and Thursday, two days). This again points to this scene being set on Thursday.

On the other hand, however, we learn that Balthasar left Verona immediately after seeing Juliet laid in the vault on Wednesday morning (V.1.20–1) and as Romeo intends to be back in Verona 'tonight' the journey between Mantua and Verona does not, according to Shakespeare, take long. Hence, Balthasar could arrive in Mantua on Wednesday, the day he seems to have left Verona. Another piece of evidence also suggests Wednesday for this scene. V.3 begins with Paris performing funeral rites at Juliet's tomb, rites he says he will perform every night hereafter (V.3.16–17). It would be natural, therefore, to suppose this is the first time he has done this, which would mean this is the first night Juliet has been in the vault, namely Wednesday. He would hardly promise to perform these rites every night on the second night he visited her tomb. And this, again, would point to our scene here as on Wednesday, since Romeo meets Paris at the Capulet vault.

In the theatre, no-one is likely to remember the Friar's forty-two hours, or notice the Watch's reference to two days. The sequence of events is clear, and the impression is of a short passage of time. Watching the play, it would seem that this scene follows immediately after IV.5, that is, that it is still Wednesday. Balthasar's comment on the haste with which he has come to Romeo (V.1.21) would reinforce this impression.

CONTEXT

Shakespeare named three of his plays after a pair of lovers: *Romeo and Juliet*; *Troilus and Cressida*; and *Antony* and *Cleopatra*. All are tragedies.

GLOSSARY

1	**If I may … sleep** if I may believe the truth of dreams which in my sleep flatter my hopes by telling me what I wish to hear
2	**presage** portend, foretell
3	**bosom's lord** i.e. heart
10–11	**how sweet … in joy** when dreams of love are so full of joy, how sweet love must be in reality
21	**presently** immediately
21	**took post** post horses were swift horses available for hire at regular intervals on main roads, and so the phrase means 'to set out quickly by horse': by the same method Romeo will return to Verona (lines 26 and 33)
28	**import** suggest, signify
29	**misadventure** tragically ill-advised undertaking
35	**see for** look for
38	**'a** he
38	**noted** noticed
39	**weeds** drab clothes
40	**Culling … simple** picking plants from which to make medicines
45	**account** collection, number
46	**bladders** used to contain liquid
47	**packthread** strong thread or twine
47	**old … roses** rose petals pressed into small tablets

GLOSSARY

51	**Whose sale ... death**	for the sale of which the penalty is immediate death
52	**caitiff wretch**	miserable or wretched creature
59	**ducats**	gold coins, each worth nearly ten shillings in Elizabethan money, so Romeo is offering nearly £20, a large sum
60	**soon-speeding gear**	quick-acting stuff
67	**any he**	any man
67	**utters**	sells
70	**starveth in thy eyes**	appear in your starving face
79	**dispatch**	kill
85	**cordial**	restorative drink (as it will restore him to Juliet)

SCENE 2

- It is explained how the letter from Friar Laurence to Romeo setting out his plan was never delivered.
- Friar Laurence must go to the vault alone.

Time: Wednesday

QUESTION
Is the use of unfortunate coincidence as a plot device a strength or weakness of the play?

Friar John explains to Friar Laurence that he has not been able to deliver to Romeo the letter explaining Friar Laurence's plan (IV.1.113–5) because he was shut up by health officers in a house in Verona which was thought to be plague-ridden. Friar Laurence must now go to the vault alone (he, of course, does not know that Romeo has also determined to go there).

COMMENTARY

This scene confirms that Romeo will not find out the truth about Juliet's 'death'. Quickly and simply things have gone terribly wrong since IV.5.

GLOSSARY

5	**bare-foot brother** friar
6	**associate** accompany; friars usually worked in pairs
8	**searchers** men who searched out the plague by checking dead bodies
10	**infectious pestilence** plague
10	**reign** ruled, that is, the inhabitants of the house were infected
11	**Sealed up the doors** confining infected people to their homes in this way this was common practice, to prevent the spread of plague
17	**brotherhood** religious order
18	**nice** trivial
18	**charge** serious matter
19	**dear import** great importance
20	**danger** damage, harm
21	**crow** crow-bar
25	**beshrew** blame
26	**accidents** doings, events, that is, Juliet's proposed marriage to Paris and the Friar's plan to prevent it

SCENE 3

- Paris, grieving at Juliet's tomb, is killed in a fight with Romeo.
- Romeo then enters the vault and poisons himself.
- When she awakes, Juliet, seeing the body of Romeo, stabs herself.
- The Friar explains these events to the appalled Montagues and Capulets, who are reconciled.

QUESTION
What would be lost were Paris to be dropped from the play?

Time: Wednesday night to near dawn on Thursday (V.3.188–9, 305–6)

The tragic catastrophe is presented in the play's final and longest scene, a scene remarkable for its variety of dramatic mood. It begins with Paris coming to grieve at Juliet's tomb. His funeral rites establish a suitably sombre mood. But Paris is disturbed by Romeo, who has arrived from Mantua to poison himself at the vault. As Romeo begins to open the tomb, Paris steps forward to stop him. Paris believes that grief for Tybalt's death, which Romeo caused, killed Juliet, and that Romeo, as a Montague, has now come to mutilate the dead bodies of the Capulets Tybalt and Juliet. Appalled by this, he attempts to arrest Romeo. In the ensuing fight, Paris is killed. This is the first time Juliet's two lovers have met on stage, and it is only after killing him that Romeo recognises Paris.

After this sudden violence, the mood changes again as Romeo opens the vault and, in a long **soliloquy**, meditates on Juliet's beauty and prepares himself for death. Just as Romeo has drunk the poison, the Friar arrives, and, finding the bodies of Paris and Romeo, he tells the waking Juliet to fly from the place. When she realises Romeo is dead, Juliet refuses to leave and stabs herself. The Watch has been summoned by Paris's servant, and there is considerable confusion as the Capulets, Montagues and the Prince are summoned and all wonder at how these three deaths can have occurred. The Friar explains what has happened, and the scene ends as Capulet and Montague are reconciled in their grief.

CHECK THE NET

Search the Net for John Everett Millais' painting, *The Death of Romeo and Juliet* (1848), which depicts the tragic final scene in the Capulet tomb.

COMMENTARY

The play had opened with a scene which brought to the stage the Capulets, Montagues and the Prince; its turning point in III.1 had again assembled these characters, and now, at the end, all are brought together once more. But whereas in I.1 and III.1 it was the continuance of their feud which had brought them together, now it is the ending of that feud and their reconciliation through the tragic deaths of their heirs, deaths for which, as the Prince himself says as the scene draws to a close, they and their hatred were responsible.

GLOSSARY		
1	**aloof**	apart
3	**all along**	at full length
6	**loose**	that is, the earth is loose
11	**adventure**	dare
12	**Sweet flower**	that is, Juliet
14	**sweet**	perfumed
15	**wanting**	lacking

GLOSSARY

20	**cross**	interfere with
21	**Muffle**	hide, conceal
23	**letter**	this Romeo had written before leaving Mantua (V.1.25)
27	**course**	course of action
33	**jealous**	inquisitive, suspicious
36	**hungry**	because Death is never satisfied
39	**empty**	and therefore hungry and savage
43	**For all this same**	all the same
44	**I fear**	give me reason to be afraid of what he will do
45	**maw**	stomach
45	**womb**	belly
48	**in despite**	to spite you (by forcing more 'food' in when the 'maw' is already 'Gorged')
53	**apprehend**	arrest
54	**unhallowed**	evil
57	**thou must die**	the punishment for returning from banishment
60	**these gone**	these buried in the vault
65	**For I come … myself**	that is, with the poison to commit suicide
68	**conjuration**	literally, casting of a magic spell; Paris means that he defies Romeo's attempt to put him off by solemn words
76	**betossèd**	tossed hither and thither (by Fortune)
83	**triumphant**	glorious
84	**lantern**	windowed upper part of a building which admits light; to Romeo the vault is a lantern because it is lit by Juliet's beauty (lines 85–6)
86	**feasting presence**	festival presence chamber, that is, the room in which a monarch would receive guests and visitors
89	**keepers**	jailers
90	**A lightning before death**	a proverbial phrase, describing a sudden burst of vigour just before death
94	**ensign**	flag, banner
97	**sheet**	winding sheet in which corpses are wrapped
100	**To sunder … enemy**	to separate from his youth him who was your enemy, that is, kill myself

CHECK THE BOOK

The reconciliation of the feuding families in *Romeo and Juliet* anticipates the endings of Shakespeare's last plays, *Cymbeline*, *The Winter's Tale* and *The Tempest*.

CHECK THE FILM

To enforce the shocking tragedy of their deaths, for a fleeting moment both lovers understand what is happening in Baz Lurhmann's film *Romeo + Juliet*. Juliet's fingers stir, and her eyelids flutter as she begins to wake unnoticed by Romeo; as he drinks the poison, he sees her wake, and she sees him as he dies.

GLOSSARY

111–12	**And shake... flesh** free this body, tired of the world, from the influence of hostile stars
115	**dateless** endless, eternal
116	**conduct** conductor, that is, the poison, which Romeo here addresses
117	**desperate pilot** that is, himself
119	**true Apothecary** the Apothecary spoke the truth (in V.1.77–9)
122	**stumbled at** stumble over. There was a superstition that to stumble was a sign that what one was doing would not turn out well
124	**Bliss** the eternal bliss of salvation in heaven
125	**vainly** in vain
136	**unthrifty** unlucky
138	**dreamt** Balthasar would actually have seen this happen: perhaps he does not want to believe that what he saw is true; perhaps (remembering it is night in a graveyard) he really does think it was a dream or hallucination; or again, perhaps he is afraid to say openly that such an awful thing has happened
142	**masterless** abandoned (by their masters or owners)
143	**discoloured** stained (with blood)
145	**unkind** unnatural
148	**comfortable** comforting
152	**contagion** contagious disease, foul influence
161	**cup** Romeo had evidently poured the poison into a cup to drink it (the apothecary had said that the poison should be taken as a drink, V.1.77–8)
162	**timeless** both 'untimely' and 'endless'
163	**churl** a mean person, here used as an affectionate rebuke
166	**restorative** that is, her kiss, which will restore her to Romeo in death
173	**attach** arrest
179	**ground** cause, explanation
181	**without** without knowing the
198	**comes** comes about
203	**house** that is, sheath
207	**warns** tolls, summons
214	**untaught** ill-mannered, used here affectionately and in sad jest

GLOSSARY

215 **press before** hurry ahead of; it was bad manners to enter a room in front of a parent

218 **spring** source of a stream, and so, cause; the metaphor is carried on in 'head', the beginning of a stream, and 'descent'

219 **general** leader

221 **And let ... patience** and let patience rule us in our response to misfortune

223 **greatest** that is, the one most suspect

225 **direful** dreadful, awful

226–7 **both to ... excused** both to accuse myself and to defend myself; the Friar knows he is guilty (his scheme caused these deaths) and yet he is innocent (that was never his intention)

229 **date of breath** span or time of breath, that is, life

233 **stolen** secret

237 **You** the Friar addresses the Capulets

238 **perforce** by force

246 **form** appearance

247 **as** on

255 **closely** secretly

266 **privy** accessory, in the secret

268 **his** its

270 **We still ... holy man** despite what you have just said, we have always known you are a holy man

273 **post** great haste

280 **made your master** was your master doing

286 **make good** confirm

289 **therewithal** with that

293 **joys** children

295 **brace of kinsmen** Mercutio and Paris were both related to the Prince

297 **jointure** marriage settlement given by the groom's family to the bride (the opposite of a dowry): Capulet means that Montague's handshake is all he can ask for as a settlement for Juliet

301 **rate** high value

303 **Romeo's** that is, Romeo's statue

303 **lie** Montague is thinking of the figures carved lying on tombs

304 **glooming** dark, sad

CONTEXT

On the Prince's remark, 'All are punished' (line 295), the Romantic writer Samuel Taylor Coleridge observed: 'Poetic justice indeed!'

EXTENDED COMMENTARIES

TEXT 1 THE NURSE REMINISCES (I.3.17–49)

Even or odd, of all days in the year,
Come Lammas Eve at night shall she be fourteen.

...

I never should forget it. 'Wilt thou not, Jule?' quoth he,
And, pretty fool, it stinted and said 'Ay'.

QUESTION
To what extent is the Nurse comic or exasperating?

The Nurse and Mercutio are the two chief sources of comic energy in the play. The comedy they provide is of very different kinds. Whereas Mercutio is a verbal gamester, all mercurial wit, the Nurse is garrulously repetitive and digressive. Though he can speak at length (as in his famous Queen Mab speech, I.4.53–95), Mercutio's characteristic manner is that of quick repartee, the swift riposte. He is a master of wordplay and the deft retort, but the Nurse can never clear-sightedly get to the point: she infuriates Juliet with her inability to say anything directly and straightforwardly (for example, when she returns from Romeo in II.5). Her tendency to prolong whatever she is saying by wandering from the point, adding details, repeating herself, is well illustrated by this speech, but it illustrates also the fact that the Nurse's role in the play is not merely to supply comic relief from the tragic story of the lovers. She provides both a context for that story, and a dramatically striking and thematically revealing contrast to the experience and perceptions of Romeo and Juliet.

In the first of these functions, she keeps before the audience the everyday facts of life. Romeo and Juliet are caught up in an exceptional love, prompting them to disregard the normal constraints on human behaviour. They take no care of any obligation save that of fidelity to each other. In the end, even the most fundamental human desire – to survive – has no hold on them. While they thus escape from all the ties of family and society, the Nurse is entirely caught up in them. Her speech is replete with the ordinary, inconsequential events which compose most human lives: for her, they are all that does constitute life. This is evident in her insistent references to time. Time is one thing Romeo and Juliet disregard. In their love affair, normal temporal sequences and expectations seem suspended: they fall in love when they are too young to do so, they marry before they have known each other more than a day, their marriage is over in a day. Their love is at once timeless, and moves at great speed. Their scenes together seem to be removed from the normal world, even though compelled by the onward rush of events.

This effect is sustained in large part by the Nurse. She brings noise and bustle on to the stage ('**hold thy peace**' says the exasperated Lady Capulet [line 30] in response to this speech), which, by contrast, makes the scenes between the lovers appear the calmer and quieter – havens of peacefulness. The absolute single-mindedness of the lovers and their clarity of purpose is the more striking because of the Nurse's complete lack of focus or purposefulness. She wants to chat, not to do. Whereas Romeo and Juliet seem driven by fate, the Nurse appears to have all the time in the world (she is certainly in no hurry here) and (at least until Juliet's apparent death) nothing to worry her. And yet the Nurse also reminds us insistently of time, but it is a time-scale quite different to that which affects Romeo and Juliet. In this speech, she ticks off days, months and years. Her life spans a long stretch of time, but it is a stretch marked out by birth, marriage and death (all are mentioned in this speech, which moves from Juliet's birth and weaning to her marriage, with mention of the death of the Nurse's own daughter and her husband); by Christian festivals (Lammastide); by natural events (the earthquake); and by ordinary domestic duties (weaning a child) and events (a child falling over), and household exchanges (her husband's joke). Her speech is larded with inconsequential details ('**sitting in the sun under the dovehouse wall**' [line 28] for example) which, though irrelevant (or, at least, not necessary) to what she is saying, create an everyday world never encountered in the lives of the lovers. Ordinariness, the keynote of the Nurse's experience, highlights, by contrast, the extraordinariness which characterises Romeo and Juliet's love. Her speech keeps the play rooted in the world of the audience's experience and epitomises the life that Romeo and Juliet will never have.

And as she talks of these things, she exemplifies values which are quite at odds with those of the hero and heroine. Her whole speech revolves around a joke about sex. She clearly enjoys the joke

> **CONTEXT**
>
> The eighteenth-century writer, Samuel Johnson, remarked that in the Nurse Shakespeare had, 'with great subtlety', drawn a character 'at once loquacious and secret, obsequious and insolent, trusty and dishonest'.

CHECK THE BOOK

Eric Partridge, *Shakespeare's Bawdy* is the best source of reference to understand Shakespeare's use of innuendo, *double entendre*, sexual imagery and bawdy puns and jokes.

hugely, just as she does sex. The love of Romeo and Juliet is certainly sexual, but their tone is never like this. They speak of and to each other with a kind of awe, as though what is happening to them is almost beyond belief. The Nurse's tone is colloquially familiar, with its everyday diction ('dug', 'tetchy' [lines 27,33]), exclamations ('by my holidam', 'by th'rood' [lines 37,44]), affectionate terms ('pretty fool' [line 32]), digressions, conversational idioms ('I do bear a brain', ''Twas no need, I trow,/To bid me trudge' [lines 30,34-5]) and phrases ('That shall she, marry!', ''A was a merry man' [lines 23,41]). Just so her attitudes are entirely down to earth. She sees nothing indecorous in talking about (and talking to her social superior about) the details of weaning, nor in contemplating Juliet in bed with a man. Whereas Romeo can apostrophise both love and death in elaborate speeches, the Nurse is matter-of-fact about, and conventional in her response to, death ('She was too good for me' [line 21]) and reduces love to a sexual encounter (the 'jest' is now 'come about' [line 46] because in marriage Juliet will lie upon her back).

And yet even here we are reminded of the ominous fate brooding over the lovers. Earthquakes were regarded by Elizabethans as portents of dire events, and that earthquake which shakes the dovecote and makes the Nurse run in with Juliet would have alarmed the audience with its intimation of catastrophe in the future. Its incongruous appearance here, amongst so much that is trivial, is the more disturbing.

TEXT 2 FIRST MEETING OF ROMEO AND JULIET (I.5.93–144)

ROMEO: If I profane with my unworthiest hand
This holy shrine, the gentle sin is this.

...

NURSE: Anon, anon!
Come, let's away. The strangers all are gone.

Romeo has been persuaded, rather against his will, to attend the Capulet party by Mercutio, who hopes that the sight of other women will shake Romeo from his infatuation with Rosaline. At the end of the previous scene, Romeo's misgivings found expression in one of the play's many speeches of dire portent (I.4.106–13), but in his next speech, far from foreseeing his 'untimely death' (line 111), he is stunned by the effect upon him of his first sight of Juliet (I.5.44–53). He resolves to speak to her, and when he does so it is in the tones of adoration and with the religious imagery which he had used at line 51. He presents himself as a pilgrim approaching the shrine of a saint. This was not at all an uncommon construction in the love poetry of the time which made ready use of religious imagery. Following **Petrarch**, the woman was frequently depicted as saint, angel, or goddess, whom the male suitor approaches with expression of his unworthiness and undeserving. The rhetoric of the poetry supposes that it is the woman's part to confer blessing, mercy, grace upon the man by answering his prayer or plea. Equally conventional is the **sonnet** form upon which Romeo here embarks (see **Tragedy, on Fate and chance**). Language, genre and imagery are all at this point telling the audience that this is a moment of true love.

QUESTION
What is the significance of the many religious allusions and references in the play?

What is not conventional is the mutuality of the exchange. Ordinarily in love poetry it is the male voice that is heard; the woman may be adored, but, almost without exception, she remains silent (the poetry of John Donne illustrates this). Curiously, while the poetry appears to elevate woman, it actually deprives her of any real presence. Even in plays, the woman's role is commonly subordinate to that of the man. In Shakespeare's *Much Ado About Nothing*, for example, Claudio is allowed a voice but the woman he loves, Hero, is silent for almost the entire play. When she does speak, it is in the role of a subordinate woman, utterly at the mercy of male perceptions. In this passage, the situation is quite different. Not only does Juliet speak but she addresses Romeo as an equal.

The point is made by the structure of the dialogue. The **sonnet** upon which Romeo embarks is taken up by Juliet. They compose it together, each having first a **quatrain**, and then an exchange of lines (not quite equally, in fact; Juliet has three lines to Romeo's six). During this exchange, the image introduced by Romeo is developed by them both, with Juliet showing herself Romeo's equal in wit. She deftly turns aside his request for a kiss with the reflection that religious devotion is satisfied with touching the statue of a saint and with hands clasped in prayer, and that it is in prayer that lips express love (lines 97–102). When Romeo responds with the request that she 'let lips do what hands do' (line 103), namely, pray by touching,

Text 2 FIRST MEETING OF ROMEO AND JULIET (1.5.93–144) continued

her exquisitely poised and tactful reply turns on a pun on *move* (it was she who had introduced the pun on *palm/palmers*): she may not move to kiss him (anymore than could the statue of a saint) though moved to grant his plea. It is at the fourteenth line of the sonnet, that is, at the completion of the pattern the audience, familiar with sonnet form, would have anticipated, that they kiss. With another exchange of wit, turning now on the idea that, as Romeo has purged his sin by this act of devotion, Juliet has now to be cleansed of the sin she has received from him, they are about to kiss when this second sonnet is interrupted by the Nurse.

This exchange has thus established not only the exalted nature of their love, through the religious imagery and the formality of the sonnet, but also its mutuality: Romeo and Juliet play equal parts, they share the exchange as they share the experience. This will hold throughout the play: it is never the case that Romeo takes charge; the lovers love, and suffer, together, equally caught up in their affection, equally helpless. That helplessness is impressed upon them immediately, even at this moment of their meeting, for in the following lines each learns the identity of the other's family. It is entirely fitting that it is the Nurse, that epitome of worldliness and the everyday, who is the source of this knowledge: as she comes to them, the world imposes its constraints upon them. The exchange between Benvolio and Romeo at lines 118–20 ominously recalls the tenor of Romeo's earlier prediction (I.4.106–13); it is echoed in Juliet's line, 'My grave is like to be my wedding bed' (line 135), the first of the many associations of love and death in the play (see **Tragedy, on Juliet as the bride of death**). Thus, from its first appearance in the play, the love between Romeo and Juliet is marked out not only as exceptional but as doomed, both transcendent and at the mercy of the world. When Juliet says, 'Prodigious birth of love it is to me' (line 140), her words define this moment of meeting in terms both of birth and of death.

TEXT 3 THE FRIAR'S FIRST APPEARANCE (II.3.1–90)

FRIAR: Now, ere the sun avance his burning eye
    The day to cheer and night's dank dew to dry,
    …

ROMEO: O, let us hence! I stand on sudden haste.

FRIAR: Wisely and slow. They stumble that run fast.

This is the first appearance of the Friar and his opening **soliloquy** strikes the note he will sound throughout the play. He holds to the Elizabethan commonplace that the world constitutes a divinely ordered harmony in which all is structured, ultimately, for good. He believes further that this harmony can be reproduced in human lives if their passions and ambitions are properly tempered. Just as beneficial and malign properties are mingled in plants, so are good and evil inclinations in human beings: 'Two such opposed kings encamp them still / In man as well as herbs – grace and rude will' (lines 23–4). All things, he reflects, can be used for good, but they can also be perverted to evil ends. When the rude will – passion, obsession, overwhelming desire – comes to dominate, the result is disaster. This is exemplified in the Montague/Capulet feud: it threatens to consume people like Tybalt, and does actually kill him and Mercutio (and also Paris, who challenges Romeo as a Montague). Yet Tybalt is not a bad man; he has been '**strained**' from his good nature (line 5).

The Friar is thus the spokesperson for moderation and restraint in the play; he holds with a temperate and constant style of life. This is reflected in the quiet, humble task he is here performing, collecting plants early in the morning to make medicines. It is the noisy excess of Romeo's feelings which dismays him later in the scene, as, we learn, it has done in the past. He has, he says, rebuked Romeo 'for doting, not for loving' (line 78), that is, for the obsessiveness of his infatuation. '**They stumble that run fast**' (line 90) are the Friar's characteristic last words in the scene.

This point of view is mirrored in the way, throughout his **soliloquy**, one thought or idea is opposed to, and balanced by, another. Quite often, a line is constructed in two halves, each set against the other: 'With baleful weeds and precious-juicèd flowers' (line 4); 'What is her burying grave, that is her womb' (line 6). More strikingly, the judicious balance which the Friar is trying to maintain is enacted by the **couplets** in which he speaks. The couplet is itself founded on balance, on harmony: one line plays against the other and makes the rhyme. The pattern is completed only when the second line is brought against the first: 'For naught so vile that on the earth doth live / But to the earth some special good doth give' (lines 13–14). In this example, each line contains a single idea, the two ideas appear

CONTEXT

Monasteries and convents had been dissolved in England in the 1530s and since then the religious orders of monks and friars had been banished as part of the English Reformation. Hence no one in Shakespeare's audience would have met a friar.

contradictory, but the rhymed couplet insists that they are equally valid. It binds them together as a single point: the qualities of natural things cannot be distinguished as wholly vile or good.

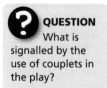

QUESTION
What is signalled by the use of couplets in the play?

The continuance of the **couplets** throughout the scene serves to define this location as the Friar's, where Romeo's is an intrusive presence. Though he does not break the couplets, he represents precisely that extremism, that excess, which the Friar disdains. Not only has he veered from one love (Rosaline) to another (Juliet) but he is even more extravagant in his second love than in his first: 'Holy Saint Francis! What a change is here!' (line 61) exclaims the Friar, and in the following lines he rehearses the extravagance of Romeo's earlier protestations and behaviour rather as Mercutio will do in the next scene (see further **The Language of Love**). The traditional behaviour of the courtly lover is reduced to absurd posturing and histrionic gestures, a matter of flighty performance, not constant commitment.

Even so, the Friar is prepared to countenance this new love in the hope it may reconcile the feuding families (lines 86–8). As this shows, there is a worldly, even political, side to him, which will lead him into plots and contrivances of dubious moral standing. The contrast with Romeo and Juliet is all to their advantage: they have a daring and a courage which is quite beyond him, and it is they, not he, who are the truly unworldly ones, even, in the end, martyrs for their love. He is, of course, right, that, 'running fast', Romeo and Juliet do 'stumble' (line 90) disastrously, but for all his common sense and prudence, the supreme image of commitment in the play is not the Friar, but the dead lovers. In the end, he is no more use to the lovers, and perhaps understands them no better than the Nurse.

PART THREE

CRITICAL APPROACHES

SHAKESPEARE'S USE OF SOURCES

Nowadays it is generally assumed that a writer should invent all his or her own work and that, once a book has been published, its text belongs to the author; no-one may copy or rework it, or lift passages from it, without permission. So it comes as something of a surprise to find that in Shakespeare's time, and for hundreds of years earlier, adapting another author's work was so far from being frowned upon that it was the usual method of composition. What was valued as original was not the invention of a new story but the inventive reworking of an old one. Hence, throughout the Middle Ages and Renaissance, stories were repeated, enlarged and embellished as they were treated again and again by writers from many countries. From the modern perspective, it appears that writers from all over Europe collaborated together over many centuries.

CHECK THE BOOK
On Shakespeare's use of sources, see Leah Scragg, *Shakespeare's Mouldy Tales*.

Romeo and Juliet exemplifies this. Shakespeare, like his contemporary dramatists, seldom invented the plots of his plays. He usually borrowed them from older poems, plays or stories, and *Romeo and Juliet* is no exception. The story had already been borrowed several times before it came to Shakespeare's turn. It was first written in Italian by Masuccio Salernitano in 1476, and was then rewritten several times by Italian and French authors during the next hundred years. In 1562 the English poet Arthur Brooke, who had read it in French and Italian, published a long poem called *The Tragicall Historye of Romeus and Juliet*. This was the main source for Shakespeare's play, but Shakespeare also knew, and used, a later English prose version of the story by William Painter. Painter included 'The goodly Historye of the true and constant love between Rhomeo and Julietta' in a collection of tales he published in 1567 called *Palace of Pleasure*. There was also an English play on this subject, which Brooke mentions in the preface to his poem. Shakespeare may very well have seen it, may even, indeed, have had a copy of it by him as he worked on his own play. If so, what he owed to it cannot be determined, as no such play has survived. His debt to Brooke's poem, however, is considerable.

CHECK THE BOOK
T.J.B. Spencer, ed., *Elizabethan Love Stories* reprints William Painter's version of 'Rhomeo and Julietta'.

This is not to say that Shakespeare was a plagiarist. The medieval and Renaissance notion of invention is to be distinguished from simple copying. Authors were expected to reshape the sources they worked with so that the result was a text new and original in its manner and its effect. Just so, Shakespeare radically changed the emphasis and structure of the story as told by Brooke.

In Brooke's poem the story lasts nine months; in Shakespeare's play it is compressed into a few days. This stresses the remarkable suddenness of the lovers' passion. It has no time to develop: it completely overwhelms Romeo and Juliet the moment they see each other. The compression of time also highlights the fragility of their love: it is no sooner experienced than it is destroyed. After their first meeting and marriage the next day, they do not have a moment of undisturbed happiness. Troubles beset them from the start and, instead of being spread over several months, they come one upon the heels of the next with no relief and no escape. Because events happen so quickly, we have a sense that the lovers are trapped, that their final deaths are inevitable (see **Plot and structure**, on **Time in the play**) and, to make the time-scale clear, the timing of each scene has been given at the beginning of each scene summary.

Only in Shakespeare's play does Paris come to Juliet's tomb. This implies in him a true affection for Juliet, but, more significantly, it enables Shakespeare to achieve a dramatically effective final scene in which Juliet's two suitors confront each other at the climax of the play. Paris has been in the background throughout the play and has, unknowingly, contributed much to the unhappiness of Juliet. Here, he too is suddenly caught up by events and destroyed by them, an unsuspecting victim of the tragedy.

CONTEXT
Mercutio's name associates him with *mercury* and is thus a clue to his quicksilver disposition.

The character of Mercutio is entirely Shakespeare's invention. In the earlier versions of the story, Mercutio plays a very small part. (For importance as a contrast to Romeo see **Characterisation**.)

Shakespeare develops the characters of the Nurse and Tybalt. This extends the range of mood and attitude in the play, and achieves a dramatically effective contrast to Juliet's character in the Nurse, while Tybalt acts as a foil for Romeo and Benvolio (see **Characterisation**).

Shakespeare makes Juliet younger. In Brooke's poem she is sixteen, but in the play she is not yet fourteen. This increases her vulnerability, but, more important, it makes more striking her development from a young and submissive girl, who is very ready to obey her parents early in the play, to a self-reliant, defiant and tragic heroine who knows her own mind at the end. By stressing her youth Shakespeare stresses this contrast between Juliet's character before and after she has met Romeo. He makes her early obedience to her parents the more credible and her later resolution to defy them the more remarkable. (For Juliet's development see **Love of Romeo and Juliet**.)

Shakespeare's poetry is a more subtle and affective (i.e. emotional) medium. This is an obvious remark, but the consequence is that in every scene the effects are more varied and more moving than in the source. To read *Romeo and Juliet* is an entirely different – and much richer – experience than reading Brooke's poem.

CHECK THE BOOK
Volume 1 of G. Bullough, ed., *Narrative and Dramatic Sources of Shakespeare* reprints Brooke's *Tragicall Historye.*

PLOT AND STRUCTURE: REALISM AND ROMANCE

SINGLE PLOT

Romeo and Juliet is firmly centred on the figures of its hero and heroine: one or other of them is nearly always on stage. There is no sub-plot, no secondary story, such as Shakespeare and other Elizabethan dramatists often introduced into their plays. It is the story of Romeo and Juliet that holds our attention throughout; the play's straightforward plot charts the course of their love. In Act I they meet; in Act II they declare their love and are secretly married; in Acts III and IV they try to overcome the obstacles in the way of their relationship, but these efforts are tragically frustrated in Act V. There is thus a clear structure: an optimistic and often comic movement up to the marriage at the end of Act II is followed by a counter-movement, which begins with the quarrel in III.1 and leads to tragedy. This clear design means that there is something relentless about the progress of the play: despite variations in mood and pace, there is no extended digression or relief from the tragic tale.

TIME IN THE PLAY

This is emphasised by the time-scale of the play. Compressing events into a few days was one of Shakespeare's most significant changes to the story as it occurred in his source (see **Shakespeare's use of sources**). As a result, the action of the play lasts only four days. From Capulet's question 'What day is this?', to which Paris replies 'Monday, my lord' (III.4.18–19), the day on which each scene occurs can be determined. What matters in the theatre, though, is not the actual day but the short time sequence. That Romeo and Juliet marry only the day after they first met is the point, not that they meet on a Sunday and marry on a Monday. Nevertheless, the names of the days are a convenient help when summarising the sequence of events, and they are used in what follows:

QUESTION
What does its time-scheme contribute to the effect of the play?

Act I opens at 9 a.m. on Sunday morning (I.1.161) and culminates in Capulet's party on Sunday evening. Act II takes us through Sunday night to dawn on Monday (II.2.176; II.3.1–2) and to the marriage of the lovers in II.6 on Monday afternoon (II.4.176–9). The quarrel that opens Act III is later on Monday afternoon (III.1.112–13), and by III.4.34–5 it is late that night. Romeo leaves Juliet in III.5 as the dawn breaks on Tuesday, and Juliet's marriage to Paris, originally planned for Thursday (III.4.17–21) is brought forward to the next day, Wednesday (IV.2.23–37). Early on Wednesday morning Juliet is discovered apparently dead (IV.5.3–4). Later that day Romeo learns, as he thinks, of Juliet's death, and that night kills himself at her tomb. The play ends as dawn is about to break on Thursday (V.3.188–9, 305–6). The play thus lasts from Sunday morning until the night of the following Wednesday/Thursday.

Such a short and consistent time-scale (even allowing for the slight difficulty about V.1 – see **Summary Act V**) is very rare in Elizabethan drama. By keeping the sequence of events clearly before the audience Shakespeare makes the tragedy the more pitiful simply because of the swiftness with which events occur. The action seems to rush on at headlong speed. 'I stand on sudden haste' says Romeo (II.3.89), and he does seem to be engaged in a race against time. Everything in the play happens at great speed. The lovers hurry into marriage, and Romeo is immediately hurried into banishment. The moment Romeo hears of Juliet's death he posts back to Verona to kill himself. In all this haste, the love of Romeo and Juliet is very short-lived. Of Romeo's avowal of love Juliet says:

> ... Although I joy in thee,
> I have no joy of this contract tonight.
> It is too rash, too unadvised, too sudden;
> Too like the lightning, which doth cease to be
> Ere one can say 'It lightens'. (II.2.116–20)

Lightning is but momentary. As Romeo prepares to kill himself he uses the word again:

> How oft when men are at the point of death
> Have they been merry! which their keepers call
> A lightning before death. O how may I
> Call this a lightning? (V.3.88–91)

Because of the time-scale of the play the love of Romeo and Juliet does seem to be a 'lightning before death'. It has no sooner come to them than it is taken from them.

COINCIDENCES AND IMPROBABILITIES IN THE ACTION

The main line of the action may be clear and the structure of the play simple, but to set down the story in bald prose may well make it sound incredible. Even if it is allowed that two young people could fall so completely in love so suddenly as do Romeo and Juliet, is it credible that they would change so completely to do so? When the play opens, Romeo is infatuated with Rosaline to an extraordinary degree. His melancholy behaviour because she rejects him is the first thing the audience learns about him (I.1.116–238) and his anguished passion is the butt of Mercutio's jokes in I.4 and II.1. For her part, Juliet, when we first meet her, has no thoughts of love or marriage, and is fully prepared to follow her parents' wishes in looking favourably on Paris (I.3.67, 98–100). And yet, in a moment, Romeo forgets Rosaline (I.5.44–53) and Juliet is thinking of marriage to an enemy (I.5.134–5). Still more improbable is the elaborate plan of Friar Laurence, involving a potion which is almost magical in its effect.

CONTEXT

Unlike his contemporary dramatists Christopher Marlowe and Ben Jonson, Shakespeare has left no record of himself in letters, contemporary accounts, notes on books or summaries of conversations or meetings.

> **CONTEXT**
>
> The tragic outcome of *Romeo and Juliet*, derived from mistakes and mischance, is very like that of the play 'Pyramus and Thisbe' comically performed in Act V of *A Midsummer Night's Dream*, written at about the same time.

On top of these central elements in the plot there is an extraordinary number of coincidences in the play, all unfortunate. That Romeo should fall in love with the daughter of an enemy house is the central, tragic, chance event. That Paris should come as suitor to Juliet at just this time is another coincidence which hastens the tragedy. That Friar Laurence's letter should not be delivered is another; that Romeo should kill himself *just before* Juliet awakes is another; that the Friar should arrive at the vault *just after* Romeo has taken poison, another. Had any of these chances fallen out differently there would have been no tragedy. Romeo, for example, would have found Juliet awake had he come a little later or she woken a little earlier. Thinking of cases like this, it is hard not to feel that Romeo and Juliet are killed by cruel chance, or fate. If Romeo's luck had been different, Friar John would have come sooner and told him the truth about Juliet's 'death'. But Romeo has no luck in this play. He and Juliet are the victims of an extraordinary succession (even an incredible succession) of mischances (see also **Tragedy**, on **Fate**).

There are other odd things about the action of the play. How can Lady Capulet know that Romeo is living in Mantua before he can possibly have arrived there and when his destination is anyway a secret (III.5.88)? When Juliet is discovered apparently dead in IV.5, why does no-one wonder why she died? No-one suspects suicide or foul play, and no-one notices the vial that must lie beside her (IV.3.20, 23). Why is it that the Friar, who expected Juliet to awake after forty-two hours (IV.1.104–5), arrives late at the vault on a matter of such urgency? How can Romeo, who has only just arrived in Mantua, have already discovered, and remembered, an apothecary's shop where he can buy poison? He had no idea he would ever need it, after all, and yet in V.1 it is immediately in his mind. Or again, why are Montagues and Capulets at each other's throats? What is the cause of their quarrel? We are never told. One last example: if we are to believe this feud stands in the way of Romeo's love for Juliet, what do we make of the fact that it did not stand in the way of his love for Rosaline? Rosaline was also a Capulet (I.2.68, 81–2), and yet Romeo had been able to see her because we know she refused him. If he could see her, why not Juliet?

Clearly, this is not a realistic text. Realism is a comparatively recent literary convention, established by the novel in the eighteenth and nineteenth centuries. Earlier literature did not attempt to depict everyday life, and therefore did not value either consistency or authenticity in its details. Hence, although *Romeo and Juliet* is set in Italy, there is no attempt to represent Italian customs accurately. Capulet's household is a typical English Elizabethan household; the masked dance at Capulet's party was fashionable in Elizabethan England and the description of the apothecary's shop (V.1.40–8) would have fitted many such shops in Elizabethan London. All through the play, proverbs, idioms and exclamations are thoroughly English. Indeed, at one point Mercutio makes fun of the Italian style of duelling which had recently become fashionable in England (II.4.19–26). This might be expected from an Englishman and it would go down well with an English audience; to object that Mercutio is supposed to be Italian, and so would never say such a thing, is beside the point. The play will not offer that kind of **verisimilitude** (likeness to reality).

QUESTION
Does the amount of coincidence in the play contribute to, or detract from, the tragedy?

THE PATTERN OF THE ACTION

Romeo and Juliet, then, does not tell a story that is correct and accurate in all its circumstantial details, believable in all its incidents. There is a story running through the whole play, and in a general way it holds together, but the kind of questions posed a moment ago cannot be answered because Shakespeare gives no answers. The reason is that the story as such is the least important part of the play. The plot is only the starting-point, the means by which characters are brought together for striking confrontations and in dramatically varied scenes. How they get there does not interest Shakespeare nearly so much as the scenes themselves. The very characters themselves are chosen not as 'real' human beings, but to contrast and complement each other in effective ways (see **Characterisation**). However we may quibble about the story of the lovers, when Romeo and Juliet speak to each other in II.2 there is no doubting the persuasiveness of their love. It is for such moments as that expression of genuine love that the plot exists.

What structures the play is, hence, not a plausible plot but a succession of complementary and contrasting incidents and scenes (such as are noticed in the scene summaries). *Romeo and Juliet* is a

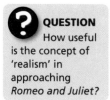

QUESTION
How useful is the concept of 'realism' in approaching *Romeo and Juliet*?

tragedy, but it is also, in performance, a play of remarkably varied moods and actions, all carefully contrived. The very first scene illustrates how the whole play works. It begins with comedy from the servants, but the mood quickly changes and there is a fight and a riot, with citizens pouring onto the stage shouting and fighting. This uproar is suddenly silenced by the appearance of the Prince who, in another change of mood, delivers an impressive and threatening long speech to his subjects. The stage then clears for new matter in a different tone. It is a family discussion about the peculiar behaviour of Romeo. When he comes on, the scene ends as it had begun, with only two people talking, but now it is not the bawdy talk of the servants we hear but the sophisticated language of love. In only just over 200 lines, Shakespeare has provided merriment, spectacle and unease; and he has also, of course, set the scene for the play. In just this way the audience's interest is maintained throughout the play. The quiet scene, II.6, is followed by the violence of III.1; Juliet's **soliloquy** in IV.3 contrasts with the bustle of IV.4; the comedy of the musicians which ends IV.5 contrasts with the outcries of grief earlier in that scene. Examples could be multiplied.

Such manipulation of the sequence of the action makes for a variety of mood and incident; it also makes for unpredictability: the audience is never quite sure what to expect next. Above all, it makes for the dramatic and poetic exploration of themes and situations which bear upon the audience's experience, despite the play's neglect of realism. *Romeo and Juliet* is a romantic tale of love which does not belong to the ordinary everyday world of cause and effect, but this is not to say that the play is merely romance in the sense of a fanciful piece of art irrelevant to our lives.

THEMES: LOVE AND HATE

THE LOVE OF ROMEO AND JULIET

Love has a transforming effect upon both Romeo and Juliet. At the beginning of the play, Romeo is a rather tiresome young man, endlessly complaining, in the elaborate language of love then fashionable, about his sorrows because Rosaline rejects him. He is playing the part of the Petrarchan lover. The love poetry of the medieval Italian poet Francesco **Petrarch** (1304–74) was widely imitated throughout the Renaissance. It established literary conventions of how to behave and how to talk when in love. In Elizabethan love poetry we meet, over and over again, lovers who behave just like Romeo. They dote upon one lady; live only for her; express their feelings in elaborate **conceits** and rhetorical phrases; they are devastated if she frowns on them and overwhelmed by joy if she smiles. It is an elaborate, exaggerated ideal, almost a religion of love.

Mercutio recognises the fashionable posturing of Romeo's behaviour when he says 'Now is he for the numbers that Petrarch flowed in' (II.4.38–9). So Romeo regards Rosaline as beyond all women in beauty: 'The all-seeing sun / Ne'er saw her match since first the world begun.' (I.2.91–2).

And he swears his love for her in religious terms – he worships her, and resorts to ingenious imagery to say so (for example I.2.87–90). He talks of his depression at her rejection of him in the same exaggerated way. It is difficult not to feel that he is wallowing in self-pity (for example I.1.186–94), and the **oxymorons** (combinations of words of opposite meanings) with which he endeavours to describe his feelings sound very much like contrivance:

> Why then, O brawling love, O loving hate,
> O anything, of nothing first create!
> O heavy lightness, serious vanity,
> Misshapen chaos of well-seeming forms,
> Feather of lead, bright smoke, cold fire, sick health,
> Still-waking sleep, that is not what it is! (1.1.176–81)

There is much to be said for the idea that Romeo is in love with the idea of being in love, and an audience is likely to have a good deal of sympathy with Benvolio's attempts to make Romeo see sense and Mercutio's efforts to mock him from his moanings. On stage the sight of neither of Romeo's two friends taking his 'love' too seriously would strengthen and audience's suspicions that this is a very young man playing love games.

When Romeo sees Juliet, the character of his extravagant avowals changes. The speech in which he first sees her has a new tenderness and awe in it:

CHECK THE BOOK

On the different ways Romeo and Juliet talk of love, see Edward Snow's essay on 'Language and Sexual Difference' in *Romeo and Juliet'* in Peter Erickson and Coppélia Kahn, eds, *Rough Magic*, 1985.

> O, she doth teach the torches to burn bright!
> It seems she hangs upon the cheek of night
> As a rich jewel in an Ethiop's ear -
> Beauty too rich for use, for earth too dear!
> So shows a snowy dove trooping with crows
> As yonder lady o'er her fellows shows ...
> Did my heart love till now? Forswear it, sight!
> For I ne'er saw true beauty till this night. (I.5.44–53)

That last line is a confession that all he said before was wrongheaded. **Ironically**, Benvolio had told Romeo that if he went to Capulet's party and saw Rosaline in the company of other ladies, he would realise she was not at all exceptional (I.2.93–8). Rosaline is indeed displaced, but by a deeper affection than Benvolio ever expected. The Friar is later amazed at Romeo's fickleness (II.3.61–76), but this is not the simple fickleness of a man exchanging one shallow love for another. It is a change from a shallow affection to a binding love. Although Romeo is always prone to lapse again into extravagant language, there is no doubting the new depth of his feelings. He is, after all, constant to Juliet to death. Shakespeare stresses this change by making Rosaline only a name. We cannot take too seriously protestations of love for a woman we never see or hear.

Juliet is never posturingly foolish in the way of Romeo but she, too, undergoes a change. At the beginning of the play she is modest, subdued and quiet. When her mother suggests that Paris might make a good husband, she simply replies:

> I'll look to like, if looking liking move.
> But no more deep will I endart mine eye
> Than your consent gives strength to make it fly. (I.3.98–100)

She is prepared to be guided entirely by her parents. For Juliet, the meeting with Romeo is an awakening to the fact that love is more than filial obedience, and with this she discovers a new resolution. She flatly contradicts her promise of obedience by marrying Romeo secretly. And she emerges as a strong and practical personality – far more so than Romeo. In the balcony scene, she addresses Romeo

CHECK THE FILM

In John Madden's 1998 film, *Shakespeare in Love*, which starred Gwyneth Paltrow and Joseph Fiennes, Shakespeare develops the plot of *Romeo and Juliet* as an expression of his own doomed (and fictional) love affair.

directly and plainly, asking down-to-earth questions to which
Romeo replies with elaborate images (for example II.2.62–9). When
she discovers that Romeo has overheard her confessing her love for
him, she does not deny it, but with startling and winning directness
dismisses the conventions of courtship: 'Fain would I dwell on form
– fain, fain deny / What I have spoke. But farewell compliment!'
(II.2.88–9). Shakespeare admired this kind of honesty: it appears in
other heroines of his (for example, Miranda in *The Tempest*,
III.1.48–91). And it is Juliet, we notice, who first mentions marriage,
and sets Romeo on to arrange it (II.2.143–8). (For Juliet's plain
language, see **The Language of Love**.) No less than Romeo's, her
commitment is absolute and unconditional, quite heedless of social
convention and family ties.

COMPETING VIEWS OF LOVE

The love of Romeo and Juliet is at odds with the world in which
they find themselves, but the play does not straightforwardly
oppose admirable lovers and detestable inhabitants of Verona. The
other characters in the play are not without sympathetic qualities,
nor are their views deprived of cogency. On the contrary, it is
through these characters, none of whom can simply be dismissed,
that the love of Romeo and Juliet is interrogated.

Juliet's father, Capulet, is a case in point. Were he simply overbearing
and tyrannical, Juliet's disobedience could be applauded. He is
certainly very cruel to Juliet in III.5, but that is not all there is to him.
He is so angry then because he is bitterly disappointed. We know he
has great affection for his daughter and hopes she will have a happy
future (I.2.7–19). He believes she grieves for the death of her cousin
Tybalt, and thinks that marriage to Paris will make her happy. This is
why he agrees to the marriage without consulting her (III.4.12–28), as
Juliet's mother says and Paris later explains to the Friar (III.5.107–10;
IV.1.6–15). He is angry when Juliet refuses in III.5 because his plans
for her happiness are frustrated. Capulet is not simply a cruel father, a
tyrant over his daughter. The audience is consequently aware of what
can be said on his part, and that Juliet does wrong in going against
him. There is some sympathy for him both when he thinks Juliet is
dead (IV.5) and when she really is so (V.3).

> **CONTEXT**
>
> The Romantic
> writer, Samuel
> Taylor Coleridge,
> described Capulet
> as 'a worthy,
> noble-minded old
> man of high rank,
> with all the
> impatience that is
> likely to
> accompany it'.

It is not, then, the case that Shakespeare surrounds two ideal lovers with unfeeling and unpleasant people, who alienate the audience. The lovers are not simply set in opposition to wrongheaded and malevolent friends and relatives. Rather, they are set among well-intentioned people who each have their own ideas on the nature of love. As a result, the love of Romeo and Juliet is only one among several kinds of love articulated in the play. *Romeo and Juliet* is a play about two young lovers in conflict with their parents and families, but it is also a play about competing ideas of love.

ROMANTIC AND UNROMANTIC LOVE

Among these are romantic and unromantic ideas of love. Romeo and Juliet are romantic. They give their all and disregard everything else. For Capulet, however, love and marriage are matters to be decided by a prudent father with the best interests of his daughter at heart. For Lady Capulet, Juliet's mother, they seem to be matters of worldly wisdom. She is a rather curt, sharp woman. She is only about twenty-eight years old (in I.3.72–4 she says she was a mother at about Juliet's age, and Juliet is now nearly fourteen), yet her husband is an old man (I.1.90; I.2.3; I.5.22–5), well past the age for dancing (I.5.31–41). To him, Lady Capulet speaks abruptly, often reminding him of his age (for example I.1.76). She seems to have little love for him in the romantic sense (for example IV.4.11–12) and the difference in their ages leads to the suspicion that it was an arranged marriage – a sensible move in order to achieve a good position in the world. Like Capulet himself, she has no patience with Juliet's refusal of her father's prudent scheme (III.5.203–4). Because of their views on love, neither parent can understand why Juliet should possibly want to decline such a handsome offer of marriage as is proposed with Paris.

In a different way, Benvolio is also sensible in his approach to love. In the early scenes of the play he tries to show Romeo that his affection for Rosaline is extravagant and unwarranted. He points out that if Romeo were to see her with other women he would realise she is nothing exceptional (I.2.85–6, 93–8). He does not treat Romeo's affection quite seriously, and wonders that Romeo can go through such agonies. That Romeo's affection for Rosaline is not genuine does not affect the common sense of what Benvolio says. He would almost certainly have said the same thing about Romeo's love for Juliet, had he known of it.

CONTEXT

For another dramatic treatment of a love which disregards all constraints and restraints, see Shakespeare's tragedy *Antony and Cleopatra*.

SPIRITUAL AND SEXUAL LOVE

Shakespeare, then, gives us prudent, sensible, worldly wise attitudes to love, from people who have Romeo's best interests at heart. So, too, there are realistic and earthy attitudes to love in conflict with more spiritual ideals. The amount of bawdy talk – the number of jokes about and references to sex – is a striking feature of the play. This is, indeed, how it begins, with Sampson and Gregory making ribald jests about male erections and taking women's virginity. For these servants, the relationships between men and women are clearly a matter of sex only. Throughout the play the love of Romeo and Juliet is set in a context of such lewd talk which has no time for notions of love. The Nurse is forever making sexual puns and innuendoes. She repeats with relish her husband's joke when the baby Juliet falls down:

> ''A was a merry man – took up the child.
> 'Yea,' quoth he, 'dost thou fall upon thy face?
> Thou wilt fall backward when thou hast more wit.
> Wilt thou not, Jule?' (I.3.41–4)

The point of the joke is, of course, that Juliet will lie on her back when a man makes love to her. The Nurse anticipates the sexual pleasures of Juliet's wedding night with Romeo (II.5.75) and with Paris (IV.5.5–7) with the same glee. Indeed, that the Nurse can suggest that Juliet should go ahead and marry Paris even though she is already married to Romeo (III.5.213–26) shows that the Nurse has scant regard for loyalty or any of the usual virtues of love. Morality and high feeling mean little to her – she sees sex as the essential thing in the relationship between men and women. Certainly the love between Juliet and Romeo is sexually consummated (and only a day after they have first met), but it is not the insatiability of sexual desire which drives them together. Sexuality is a part, not the essence, of their relationship; it is the expression of a love which involves more than desire, and not the whole point of love, as it is for the Nurse.

Mercutio, too, has little patience with Romeo's high feelings. He has a down-to-earth remedy for Romeo: 'If love be rough with you, be rough with love' (I.4.27). He cannot see the sense of Romeo's 'dumps' and by his jokes constantly makes fun of Romeo's

 CHECK THE BOOK
Joseph A. Porter, *Shakespeare's Mercutio: his History and Drama*, 1988, is a book-length account of this character.

COMPETING VIEWS OF LOVE continued

pretensions. He mocks Romeo's extravagant passion (II.1.6–21), and by his insinuations suggests it is all a fraud to disguise simple sexual passion (II.1.33–8). Again, the point should be made that these are the views of characters who hold Juliet and Romeo dear; they cannot simply be dismissed as malevolent or unfeeling.

PASSION AND MODERATION

Another opposition is that between passion and moderation. The Friar, who as 'ghostly father' (II.2.192) to both Romeo and Juliet is much concerned for their spiritual welfare, often speaks against uncontrolled passion. It was, he says, that Romeo 'doted' (II.3.78) on Rosaline, not that he 'loved' her, which he disapproved of (II.3.77–8). That is, he disapproved of unreasonable infatuation ('doting'), not what he calls 'love'. But, clearly, for the Friar love is a thing of moderation. Feelings should always be controlled. He does not like the sudden haste of the impetuous lover Romeo – 'Wisely and slow. They stumble that run fast' (II.3.90) – and is suspicious of great passion:

> These violent delights have violent ends
> And in their triumph die, like fire and powder,
> Which as they kiss consume. (II.6.9–11)

He directs Romeo to 'love moderately'. Such a love, he believes, will last (II.6.14–15).

WERE ROMEO AND JULIET WRONG?

These, then, are some of the conflicting attitudes to love in the play. The hero and heroine are surrounded not by people who, all in their different ways, advise against extreme passion and unconsidered love. Their advice makes sense, the more so when we remember that Juliet herself was half-afraid that what the lovers experience was too sudden to be sincere (II.2.116–20). And in one way, of course, everyone else in the play is right. The romantic love of Romeo and Juliet does lead to their death. It is quite true that they act without forethought, without consideration of the consequences, that they are consumed by their love, and that the result is that they die. And to an Elizabethan audience it would have been plainer than it perhaps is to modern spectators that Romeo and Juliet did wrong to

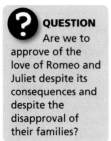

QUESTION
Are we to approve of the love of Romeo and Juliet despite its consequences and despite the disapproval of their families?

marry in secret without their parents' consent. This would have
been a serious act of disobedience at that time. Indeed, Arthur
Brooke had seen this as the point of the tragedy. In the preface to
his poem, he explained that he believes Romeo and Juliet were justly
punished for their immoderate passion and their defiance of proper
authority in arranging a secret marriage. Brooke calls their love
'unhonest desire', and rebukes Romeo and Juliet for ignoring their
parents and making use of 'dronken gosyppes' and 'superstitious
friers' in order to satisfy their 'wished lust'. To his mind, they
shamefully abused 'the honorable name of lawefull mariage' and
thoroughly deserved to die for their 'unhonest lyfe'.

Is this the import of Shakespeare's play? Do Romeo and Juliet
deserve the criticism they received from the other characters? Are
they justly punished?

THE FEUD

The answer is, no. Shakespeare's play actually inverts Brooke's
poem. His radical reworking of his source draws from it quite
another meaning. On the one hand, the attractiveness of the lovers'
characters and the poetic beauty of the scenes in which they meet
demand that an audience responds wholly and totally to their love.
On the other hand, the parents whom Romeo and Juliet defy are
engaged in a feud. The love of the hero and heroine is set in a
context of hate. This is an extremely significant point to grasp. The
play's first scene is concerned with this feud; we are made aware of
it before ever we meet Romeo or Juliet – indeed, the 'ancient
grudge' between the 'two households' is the very first thing the
Chorus mentions in the Prologue (lines 1–4). How this feud began
is never revealed (and so we cannot take sides), but throughout the
play the audience is constantly reminded of it. The 'fiery Tybalt'
(I.1.109), who appears in the first scene, is in the background
throughout the early scenes of the play. His determination not to let
the matter of Romeo's intrusion into Capulet's party drop (I.5.91–2)
raises ominous fears about what he will do. And in III.1, the
turning-point of the play, the worst comes about. The feud is
directly responsible for the secret marriage, Romeo's banishment,
and so for the Friar's scheme which leads to the deaths of the lovers.
In short, it is hate which kills Romeo and Juliet in Shakespeare's
play. It is only because they belong to enemy families that all the

**CHECK
THE FILM**
Both *West Side
Story* and Baz
Lurhmann's *Romeo
+ Juliet* present the
feud between the
Montagues and the
Capulets in terms of
modern urban
gangland rivalry.

CHECK THE FILM

In his film of *Romeo and Juliet*, Zeffirelli presents the fight between Mercuito and Tybalt as a kind of comical mock-heroic combat in which neither seriously intends to harm the other, nor do the onlookers realise that Mercutio has been seriously wounded following Romeo's intervention. The sudden eruption of tragedy out of comedy is unforeseen and unexpected.

apprehension and secrecy are necessary. And only because of that do things go so badly wrong.

It is now clearer why the play devotes so much space to this feud: it is the feud which vindicates Romeo and Juliet in their rejection of all social and familial ties for love. Everyone else in the play may be full of good sense about love, but they are all also obsessively hostile to each other, enslaved to hatred. This fatally flaws everything they say on the subject, for it is evident that the capacity to move beyond prejudice is quite beyond them. Romeo and Juliet alone are not subject to this obsession. They alone have escaped. They want nothing to do with the feud. Romeo clearly does his very best not to become involved in III.1. Shakespeare here makes an effective alteration to the story as told in Brooke's poem. There, Romeo and Tybalt alone fight. By making Romeo refuse, only to be drawn in by the death of his friend Mercutio, Shakespeare makes it plain that Romeo was an unwilling combatant. In short, the world of Romeo and Juliet's love, in II.2 and III.5, seems a haven of peace and love, removed from all this brawling and hate.

THE TRIUMPH OF LOVE

This haven is very short-lived and cruelly destroyed. There is no escaping the senseless horror of that, but neither is that a complete account of the play's ending. The Prince tries to stop the feuding, but in vain; the Friar hopes that the marriage of Romeo and Juliet may unite the families, but his scheme goes terribly wrong. Neither the Church (the Friar) nor the State (the Prince), with all their worldly wisdom, all their common sense, can end the hatred. But the love of Romeo and Juliet can. The awful, tragic price to be paid is their deaths, but for this the responsibility lies not with them but with the Montagues and Capulets. And it is their deaths, compelling Capulet and Montague to recognise how wickedly foolish is their feud, which reconcile them. In this respect, the last 150 lines of the play, following the deaths of Romeo and Juliet, which might seem an anti-climax, are crucial. It is here that the redemptive work of the tragedy is achieved. As the Friar explains at length the tricks and deceits Romeo and Juliet had been put to by their families' hostility for each other, shame grows in Capulet and Montague, and, realising what they have done, in their grief and guilt they are reconciled.

So the play ends not with the deaths of Romeo and Juliet, but in reconciliation. It ends with the triumph of love. To the feuding world of Verona, peace and harmony are restored by the fates of Romeo and Juliet. This is only possible (and this is the point) because Romeo and Juliet did not listen to anyone's advice. It was only because they were true to each other, that they defied the world and neglected its advice, that they were killed; and it was only because of this that hatred finally died. Had the play ended with their deaths, all would have been lost; as it is, the play ends with positive gain. Had Shakespeare not dwelt on the feud, the play would have shown love destroyed and would have been an unrelievedly pessimistic play. As it is, though love is destroyed, it is not destroyed in vain. The price to be paid is very high – we may feel, too high – as it always is in tragedy, but this is not a play only about loss. Its drift is to demonstrate in love an ability to heal old wounds, of which no-one else's idea of love in the play has any understanding.

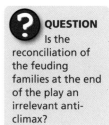

QUESTION
Is the reconciliation of the feuding families at the end of the play an irrelevant anti-climax?

TRAGEDY: FOREBODING AND FATE

This brings us to the essential paradox of tragedy, or, at least, of Shakespearean tragedy, that, despite its appalling sadness, it holds gain and loss in an unresolved tension. Shakespeare's tragedies can be almost unbearably grim in their injustice (no-one could argue that Romeo and Juliet deserve to die), but they are not straightforwardly pessimistic, hopeless plays. *Romeo and Juliet* vindicates the lovers even as it destroys them. Their love brings about reconciliation and peace at the terrible cost of their deaths. The play generates both relief that they did not die in vain, and overwhelming sadness that they had to die at all. The two things go hand in hand: it is because Romeo and Juliet are the lovers they are that they deserve life, and yet it is precisely because they are the lovers they are that they have to die. The point can be put the other way around: were they not such lovers they would have lived, but then, their love would hardly have been remarkable and could have had no regenerating effect; the feud would have continued too. It would have been a much sadder – indeed, a hopeless – play, had Romeo and Juliet submitted and decided never to see each other again. This is the central **irony** of Shakespearean tragedy: the audience suffers because it so much wants a happy ending even it knows that this is impossible, that, in some awful way, it is better that the protagonists die.

TRAGEDY: FOREBODING AND FATE

INEVITABILITY IN THE PLAY

In *Romeo and Juliet* it is quite clear that the lovers do have to die, that they are doomed. Shakespeare's conception of tragedy in this early play depicts the lovers as the victims of circumstances. They are not responsible for their fates: a terrible succession of mischances destroys them. Had any one of so many things been different, all would have been well. Had Friar Laurence's letter been delivered … had Juliet woken earlier … and so on. These coincidences are hardly realistic (see **Coincidences … in the Action**), but they do serve an important dramatic purpose: the fact that things keep going against the lovers creates the impression that a hostile and malign fate is at work. This view is encouraged throughout the play.

Right at the start, the Chorus announces that we are to see a 'pair of star-crossed lovers' (line 6) and from then on there are repeated ominous suggestions that Romeo and Juliet are fated to die. Even before Romeo has seen Juliet, as he is about to join Capulet's party he says:

> … my mind misgives
> Some consequence, yet hanging in the stars,
> Shall bitterly begin his fearful date
> With this night's revels and expire the term
> Of a despised life, closed in my breast,
> By some vile forfeit of untimely death. (I.4.106–11)

He is, of course, right, and the audience, hearing these lines, fears as much. The moment after they have met, each lover has a similar foreboding that this love will end in disaster. When Benvolio says, 'Away, be gone. The sport is at the best', Romeo replies, 'Ay, so I fear', meaning he fears things can only get worse from now on (I.5.119–20). And Juliet, learning Romeo's identity from the Nurse, says 'Prodigious birth of love it is to me / That I must love a loathed enemy' (I.5.140–1). In the balcony scene, when they declare their love, Juliet mistrusts this sudden passion (II.2.116–20). Romeo goes to marry Juliet with a challenge to fate on his lips – 'Then love-devouring death do what he dare' (II.6.7) – and an Elizabethan audience would know that fate has a habit of accepting such challenges. As the lovers part, Juliet asks Romeo 'O, thinkest thou we shall ever meet again?'; Romeo tries to reassure her, but she replies:

> O God, I have an ill-divining soul!
> Methinks I see thee, now thou art so low,
> As one dead in the bottom of a tomb. (III.5.54–6)

The next time she sees Romeo he is, indeed, dead in the bottom of a tomb. Romeo's dream, which he recounts as he waits in Mantua for news from Verona, has a similarly ominous note: 'I dreamt my lady came and found me dead' (V.1.6). When Romeo hears the news of Juliet's death, he turns on fate: 'I defy you, stars' he cries (V.1.24). As he looks on the dead Paris, he thinks of the two of them as the victims of circumstances, both written 'in sour misfortune's book' (V.3.82), and, as he prepares to kill himself, he says he will 'shake the yoke of inauspicious stars / From this world-wearied flesh' (V.3.111–12). And the Friar himself, who had tried to help these 'star-crossed' lovers, admits there was nothing he could do against the fate which seems to have worked against them: 'A greater power than we can contradict / Hath thwarted our intents' (V.3.153–4).

References like these throughout the play steadily increase the air of foreboding and strengthen the impression, which the sad succession of hostile chances has given, that there is nothing Romeo and Juliet can do. They seem helpless. The curse of a dying man was, to Elizabethans, particularly ominous, and the dying Mercutio cries three times 'A plague a'both your houses' (III.1.91, 99–100, 108). The point is plain.

JULIET AS THE BRIDE OF DEATH

One recurring kind of remark works particularly strongly to darken the atmosphere of the play. Time and again Shakespeare introduces the idea that Juliet will be the bride of Death. She herself first speaks like this the moment after she has first met Romeo: 'Go ask his name. – If he be married, / My grave is like to be my wedding bed' (I.5.134–5). When she hears of Romeo's banishment she looks at the ropes which were to have brought Romeo to her room, and resolves:

> He made you for a highway to my bed,
> But I, a maid, die maiden-widowèd.
> Come, cords. Come, Nurse. I'll to my wedding bed,
> And death, not Romeo, take my maidenhead. (III.2.134–7)

? QUESTION
How far is it adequate to see *Romeo and Juliet* as a dramatisation of adolescent passion?

Lady Capulet reminds the audience of this way of thinking about Juliet when she exclaims, in her anger at Juliet's refusal to marry Paris, 'I would the fool were married to her grave' (III.5.140), and Juliet's father, Capulet, speaks similarly when he thinks Juliet is dead:

> Death is my son-in-law. Death is my heir.
> My daughter he hath wedded. I will die
> And leave him all. Life, living, all is death's. (IV.5.38–40)

Paris, weeping at the vault, thinks that he grieves by Juliet's bridal bed (V.3.12), and finally, Romeo, preparing to join Juliet in death, and seeing her beauty, thinks Death loves her and this keeps her beautiful:

> ... Ah, dear Juliet,
> Why art thou yet so fair? Shall I believe
> That unsubstantial death is amorous,
> And that the lean abhorrèd monster keeps
> Thee here in dark to be his paramour? (V.3.101–5)

Remarks like these mean that death is always in the back of the minds of the audience; they encourage us to expect it to be the result of the lovers' affair and so impress on us the hopelessness of their situation.

FATE AND CHANCE

QUESTION Has the concept of justice any relevance to *Romeo and Juliet*?

In this play, then, Shakespeare's idea of tragedy is of a hostile fate working against the lovers. Through no fault of their own, circumstances are repeatedly arranged to work against them. This is the old medieval idea of tragedy. In his later tragedies Shakespeare made it more problematic through introducing more complex causes that involve the aspirations, choices and misconceptions of the tragic protagonists themselves. In plays like *King Lear* and *Othello*, though the tragic heroes are both the victims of hostile circumstances, they are also complicit in their tragedies in a way that is not true of Romeo and Juliet. To a degree, Lear brings his death upon himself, through his pride, his indolence, his passion, his prejudice. It is Othello's vulnerability to Iago's false suggestion that his wife, Desdemona, is unfaithful, that kills both him and her. That vulnerability is a construction of personal, social, political and sexual features far more complex than anything in *Romeo and Juliet*.

In *Romeo and Juliet*, chance is paramount. Romeo's impetuosity may contribute something to the tragedy (see **Characterisation**), but the marriage is not a wrong decision, whereas Othello was simply wrong to believe that Desdemona was unfaithful. It may have been an unwise decision to get married, but the price they pay far exceeds what that should incur. It is fate which determines that the lovers should be born of enemy families, that Mercutio should be killed by Tybalt, that Friar Laurence's letter should not be delivered. This is what destroys them; they are to be pitied as innocent victims.

> **CONTEXT**
>
> In the view of the eighteenth-century writer Samuel Johnson, 'a quibble was to Shakespeare the Fatal Cleopatra for which he lost the world, and was content to lose it'.

This is certainly how Romeo and Juliet speak of themselves. After killing Tybalt Romeo exclaims 'O, I am fortune's fool' (III.1.136), and later he speaks of his 'betossed soul' (V.3.76), suggesting that, like a helpless ship in a storm, he is blown hither and thither by fate. And when she learns she must marry Paris Juliet exclaims in despair that she is the weak victim of fate's schemes: 'Alack, alack, that heaven should practise stratagems / Upon so soft a subject as myself!' (III.5.210–11). Shakespeare's presentation thus invites sympathy, and is quite unlike the moral indignation of his source, the poem by Brooke (see **Themes on Were Romeo and Juliet wrong?**).

STYLE: WORDPLAY AND PLAIN SPEAKING

LINGUISTIC CHANGES

On first reading, the words on the page of a Shakespeare play, particularly one like *Romeo and Juliet*, can seem very odd indeed. This is explicable partly in terms of linguistic change during the 400 years since Shakespeare wrote; words change their senses, colloquial expressions go out of fashion, idioms alter. Often a curious-looking line in Shakespeare can be explained in this way. The very first line of *Romeo and Juliet* is an example: 'Gregory, on my word, we'll not carry coals'. Sampson and Gregory do not put a sack of coals down on the stage in disgust, nor does Sampson mean that he is not going to fetch any for Capulet. He is using a proverbial expression which has now fallen into disuse: his meaning is that he is not going to put up with any insults from the Montagues. On first appearance, Mercutio's remark to Romeo, 'Tut, dun's the mouse, the constable's own word' (I.4.40), looks very like nonsense. Again, Mercutio is using a colloquialism that has gone out of fashion. His meaning is simply 'be quiet', 'stop talking like that'.

A greater risk of misinterpretation is posed by words and phrases which look familiar enough, for the meanings of many words still in use have changed since Elizabethan times. Consequently, many lines which appear to make good sense actually carry a meaning quite contrary to the sense we take from them. When Tybalt is angry because Romeo has come to Capulet's party, Capulet tries to calm him, and says: 'Here in my house do him no disparagement. / Therefore be patient; take no note of him' (I.5.70–1). Capulet does not mean that Tybalt should be patient, ignore Romeo now, and wait for another opportunity; he means quite the opposite, that Tybalt should be calm and forget about Romeo altogether. When Juliet, in the balcony scene, says to Romeo, 'In truth, fair Montague, I am too fond' (II.2.98), a modern reader is likely to understand 'fond' to mean 'affectionate', and so suppose Juliet is saying that she likes Romeo too much. 'Fond' did have this meaning in the Elizabethan period, but it also meant 'foolish' and that meaning is not excluded here. Juliet is saying that she may seem silly in liking Romeo so much so suddenly. Unless both senses of the word 'fond' are recognised, only half the sense of the line is received.

WORDPLAY

That last example introduces another linguistic feature of the play. Juliet's line was clearly written by a man who was alive to the ambiguities of words, the different senses they carry, and who wished to use these senses. Shakespeare often carries on several meanings at once; his language is **multivocal** (speaking with more than one voice) or **multivalent** (having more than one meaning). He delights in ambiguities, in the connotations and nuances of words. Particularly in an early play like *Romeo and Juliet* there is a kind of exuberance, of abandon, in the manipulation of words. The text abounds with examples of the rhetorical and **metaphorical** ingenuity which the Elizabethans applauded as 'witty writing'. (**Elizabethan wit** conveyed far more than humour, though this might be part of its effect; it contained the idea of surprise and unexpectedness, with a touch of fantasticality. In modern English it might be rendered as clever inventiveness, ingenious dexterity). This can be very disconcerting for a modern reader unaccustomed to this taste for elaboration, repetition, puns, paradoxes, **conceits**.

CHECK THE BOOK

M.M. Mahood, *Shakespeare's Wordplay* discusses Shakespeare's quibbles and puns, with examples from *Romeo and Juliet*.

This is most immediately evident in the wordplay in which everyone in *Romeo and Juliet* indulges. Characters quibble with words, play with their senses, make puns, from the very first lines of the play, when the servants talk about 'coals', 'collier', 'choler' and 'collar', until its end, when the Prince speaks of heaven finding means 'to kill your joys with love' and of a 'glooming peace' (V.3.293, 305). Unfamiliarity with the vocabulary and literary manner makes it very difficult to follow such a 'wit combat' as Romeo and Mercutio's in II.4. Mercutio is the character most adept at playing with double meanings. Romeo cannot say the simplest thing without Mercutio twisting it. Romeo, though, can do it too. When Mercutio observes that 'dreamers often lie', that is that they tell lies, Romeo wittily follows by taking 'lie' in the sense 'lie down' when he says 'In bed asleep, while they do dream things true'. Mercutio had made a complete statement; Romeo uses it as merely the introduction to his own point, which is the opposite of Mercutio's. And he does this simply by a play on the word 'lie' (I.4.51–2).

What is the point of such wordplay? Part of the answer is that in the pun, the quibble, double meanings and the like, Shakespeare was displaying his skill. He was a professional writer, responding to the taste of his audience (and, we may conjecture, himself). Elizabethans greatly appreciated this kind of linguistic ingenuity. The love poetry of John Donne, written at the same time as *Romeo and Juliet*, is characterised by the same kind of exhibitionist wordplay. The intention is to call attention to the writing itself. In that respect, the text of *Romeo and Juliet* is not a means to an end. It is not simply the medium by which the characters speak and the action is realised. It is itself an end, to be enjoyed for its own sake, regardless of what it conveys about character or plot.

> **CONTEXT**
>
> The *Songs and Sonnets* of John Donne contain the most inventive and dramatic love poetry of the Renaissance.

Modern taste can accept the comic use of the pun but can be disconcerted when Shakespeare indulges in verbal ingenuity at serious moments. Sometimes it is very hard to see how the puns in such cases contribute to the effect. When Juliet is saying goodbye to Romeo she puns on the word 'division' (III.5.29–30). Her feelings are genuine in this passage, but to modern taste the wordplay introduces a note of false ingenuity.

In some serious moments, though, it is clear how the wordplay contributes to the effect. It may produce powerful compression of language: much is said in little space. For example, when the Prince says 'Throw your mistempered weapons to the ground' (I.1.87), he means that the weapons are badly tempered (or made) because they are used in bad temper by fellow citizens against each other. Or it may express confusion of feeling: when Juliet fears Romeo is dead, she puns on the pronoun 'I', the vowel 'i', the eye and the word 'ay' (III.2.45–50). Her lines effectively convey the fact that if Romeo is dead she too ceases to exist as a person, as a distinct 'I'. Later in this scene, Juliet strings together a list of **oxymorons** (III.2.75–6). The verbal conflict in these words of opposite meanings reflects Juliet's emotional conflict: she loves Romeo and yet is appalled at what he has done in killing Tybalt. In III.5, after Romeo has left, Lady Capulet comes to speak to Juliet. She believes Juliet grieves for the death of Tybalt, though we know Juliet is actually grieving for Romeo's departure. The two understandings are kept in play throughout the dialogue, Juliet meaning one thing and Lady Capulet taking a different meaning. Here, the verbal ingenuity underlines the gulf between mother and daughter. They are not talking to each other at all. Lady Capulet has no notion of what her daughter really means or any understanding of her true feelings, and this the audience realises since it does understand what Juliet means (III.5.68–102).

THE LANGUAGE OF LOVE

A different aspect of this delight in language is Shakespeare's use of the conventional diction of love poetry. We have noticed that Mercutio jests at Romeo as a follower of **Petrarch** (see **Love of Romeo and Juliet**), and in the early scenes Romeo is forever using an exaggerated form of the artificial language of Renaissance love poetry. The implication of the **hyperbole** (exaggeration) and contrivance of his speeches in I.1 and I.2 is that his feelings for Rosaline do not run very deep. (In a similar way, the over-obvious rhetorical patterning of the laments in IV.5.49–64 prevents us from taking them too seriously.)

But Shakespeare can use the conventions of love poetry to quite a different purpose. The **sonnet** was then the most popular form for love poetry. Sir Philip Sidney's sequence of sonnets *Astrophel and Stella* (1591) started a vogue, almost a craze. Every poet (including Shakespeare himself) turned out love sonnets during the last decade of the sixteenth century and the first of the seventeenth century.

CHECK THE BOOK

For the development of the sonnet form in the Renaissance, see Michael Spiller, *Early Modern Sonneteers*, 2001.

Shakespeare uses this form in all seriousness in the play. When Romeo and Juliet first meet, their conversation is in the form of an **Elizabethan (or Shakespearean) sonnet**. This usually rhymed *abab cdcd efef gg*, although this example (1.5.93–106) repeats the second rhyme of the first **quatrain** to give *abab cbcb dede ff*. The closing **couplet** brings it to a final climax. This sonnet gives to the meeting that the audience has been expecting a formality and dignity, as well as an elevating and lyrical quality. Just as the form of the sonnet is completed in the final couplet, so the meeting comes to a climax, the courtship is completed, and the lovers kiss.

This is, clearly, a carefully designed 'set piece'. There are a number of other such set pieces in the play, carefully written speeches, which may strike modern taste as a little over-long. Examples are Mercutio's Queen Mab speech (I.4.53–95); Juliet's **soliloquies** as she waits for news of Romeo and as she prepares to take the potion (III.2.1–31; IV.3.14–59); the Friar's first soliloquy, his long speech to Romeo on moderation and patience, his explanation of his plan and his summary of the plot (II.3.1–26; III.3.108–58; IV.1.89–120; V.3.229–69); and Romeo's soliloquy as he prepares for death (V.3.74–120). Here we are again confronted with the fact that this is not realistic drama but poetic drama, addressed to an audience who appreciated verse. The way to respond to such pieces is not to ask whether people in this situation would really have talked like this; nor is it to ask whether the point made needs to be made at such length. These are not prose passages conveying only meaning, but passages which, though poetry, seek to create a certain mood or response to what is happening. They are the Elizabethan equivalent of the photographic and sound effects a modern film producer uses to persuade his audience to respond in a certain way to his film.

? **QUESTION**
How far does the convention of the soliloquy depend upon the structure of the Elizabethan theatre for its effectiveness?

STYLISTIC VARIETY

Something of the variety of Shakespeare's style in the play is beginning to emerge. We have noticed:

- The use of colloquial idioms
- Punning for comic effect
- Wordplay for serious dramatic effect

- The use of the conventional language of love poetry, both mockingly and in earnest

- Elaborate soliloquies and long speeches

To these we may add:

THE USE OF PROSE

Shakespeare always used prose for comic characters and characters of a low position in society. So the servants, Gregory and Sampson, begin the play in prose. It obviously distinguishes them from the noble and more important characters who speak in more expressive and dignified verse. Prose is also used to show changes of feeling and mood. The comic banter at the beginning of II.4 is in prose, but later in the scene when, in more serious mood, Romeo plans his marriage, he speaks in verse. In II.5 the Nurse moves in and out of prose according to the tone of her speech; when she finally gets to the important matter of Romeo's message, she settles on verse.

THE USE OF RHYME

There is far more rhyme in this early play than in Shakespeare's later work. With the passage of time he came to use **blank verse** (unrhymed lines of five stresses) almost exclusively. Rhymed verse obviously sounds more artificial than unrhymed (we notice the rhymes), and it limits the poet, who has to find a rhyming word at the end of each line. In *Romeo and Juliet* the rhyme is often incidental, but in II.3, for example, its use throughout the scene serves to remove the world of the Friar and his cell from the rest of the play, where people do not use rhyme so consistently. Rhyme may mark out key statements (for example, III.1.119–20), and its formality of tone is used to distinguish important moments in the action, for example, when Romeo first sees Juliet (I.5.44–53) and the ending of the play. It may also register a decisive change in the action: so, when Romeo leaves Juliet, it is with a couplet (III.5.58–9). In all these cases (and many others) the rhyming words signal that something significant is happening at that moment.

SUITING OF LANGUAGE TO CHARACTER

The formality of Escalus's speeches may be contrasted with Mercutio's wit, and both of these with the Nurse's colloquial and

CHECK THE BOOK

On the connection between *Romeo and Juliet* and the sonnet vogue, see Nicholas Brooke, *Shakespeare's Early Tragedies*, 1968.

wandering utterances. Similarly, variety in the language expresses the different moods of a character: in I.2 Capulet speaks calmly, but his disjointed speech towards the end of III.5 effectively conveys the heat of his emotions.

IMAGERY

Romeo and Juliet is remarkable for the evocative power of its imagery. This is another aspect of that delight in words mentioned earlier, and again marks out the play as an early work. There is an extraordinary richness in its figurative language. This is especially noticeable in the balcony scene, II.2, but it is there, in a different mood, in Juliet's soliloquy in IV.3 and as Romeo prepares for death in V.3. Shakespeare can conjure up exquisite beauty and horrible death, the beautiful and the grotesque, with equally vivid imagery. The **metaphors** can also be more subtle: Lady Capulet's elaborate comparison of Paris to a book sounds impossibly far-fetched and contrived, and so reflects the insincerity of her feelings. She is not really interested in Paris as a person at all. She wants to 'sell' Paris to Juliet as a highly desirable husband (I.3.80–95).

WORDS AND TRUTH

There is one way in which language impinges upon the themes of the play. Throughout his career Shakespeare was intrigued by the relationship between words and truth. Often in his plays elaborate and involved language is associated with hypocrisy and deceit, plain speaking with honesty and truthfulness. In *King Lear*, for example, the daughters Goneril and Regan, who do not love their father Lear, speak to him in ornate and contrived speeches; the third daughter, Cordelia, who does love him, speaks plainly and directly. The nobleman, Kent, who sides with Cordelia when Lear casts her off, also speaks bluntly and plainly; the courtier Oswald, who sides with Goneril in her quarrel with the King, speaks in the fashionable language of the court. When Lear himself comes to realise the truth, he too speaks plainly (*King Lear*, I.1.34–187; II.2.1–122; IV.7.1–85.)

Although an early play, *Romeo and Juliet* shows something of the same bias. Mercutio mocks Romeo for adopting the language of love poetry (II.4.38–43; see **Love of Romeo and Juliet**), and Mercutio similarly mocks as false the assumed language of fashionable

> **CONTEXT**
>
> For another dramatic exploration of the relationship between truth and the postures and words of lovers, see Shakespeare's comedy *As You Like It*.

courtiers (II.4.28–35). The Friar makes a similar point. When Romeo comes to tell him of his new love for Juliet, the Friar loses patience with Romeo's elaborate **metaphorical** language, and begs Romeo, 'Be plain, good son, and homely in thy drift. / Riddling confession finds but riddling shrift' (II.3.51–2). At this Romeo at last gives over his **conceits,** and speaks directly: 'Then plainly know my heart's dear love is set / On the fair daughter of rich Capulet' (II.3.53–4). And the Friar suggests Rosaline had rejected Romeo precisely because his affected talk of love was seen by her as insincere, something memorised specially for the occasion: 'O, she knew well / Thy love did read by rote, that could not spell' (II.3.83–4).

Above all, though, it is Juliet who is suspicious of words. In the balcony scene she rejects the affected language of courtship, that is, language which does not tell the truth about one's feelings ('farewell compliment' (II.2.89)); she beseeches Romeo to speak plainly ('O gentle Romeo / If thou dost love, pronounce it faithfully' (II.2.93–4)); and she stops Romeo swearing an elaborate lover's oath (II.2.109–11). Her frankness here reflects her sincere and unaffected feelings. Later in the play, there is a clear contrast between Romeo, still inclined to be fanciful, and Juliet. As they are about to be married, Romeo asks Juliet to describe their love, as he cannot do it:

> Ah, Juliet, if the measure of thy joy
> Be heaped like mine, and that thy skill be more
> To blazon it, then sweeten with thy breath
> This neighbour air, and let rich music's tongue
> Unfold the imagined happiness that both
> Receive in either by this dear encounter. (II.6.24–9)

Romeo's language here – 'blazon', 'rich music's tongue' – shows the kind of thing he has in mind. Juliet, however, replies:

> Conceit, more rich in matter than in words,
> Brags of his substance, not of ornament.
> They are but beggars that can count their worth.
> But my true love is grown to such excess
> I cannot sum up sum of half my wealth. (II.6.30–4)

CONTEXT

Among the many musical compositions which *Romeo and Juliet* has inspired is the fantasy overture *Romeo and Juliette* by the Russian composer Piotr Tchaikovsky, first performed in Moscow in 1870 and Sergei Prokofiev's two ballet suites, first performed in 1935, as well as his *Fifth Symphony* of 1944.

Juliet is saying here that words, however elaborate, cannot possibly convey what she feels; and that she values the thing itself (her love) more than the ability to describe it. In other words, she sees Romeo's invitation as a pointless exercise. This distrust of fine-sounding words to convey anything truly will be a recurring theme in later plays.

CHARACTERISATION

THE GROUPING OF THE CHARACTERS

The action of *Romeo and Juliet* involves two carefully balanced groups of characters. At the head of the two feuding families of Verona are Lord and Lady Capulet and Lord and Lady Montague. Juliet, not yet fourteen years old (I.2.9; I.3.11–15), is the only child and heir of the Capulets (I.2.14; I.5.112–7), as the youthful Romeo is of the Montagues (we hear of no other children, and V.3.210–11 suggests Romeo is an only son). As Juliet has a cousin, Tybalt (I.5.61; III.2.66, 96), so Benvolio is Romeo's cousin (I.1.105, 159; II.1.3). These two cousins are clearly contrasted. When we first meet them, Tybalt starts a fight and Benvolio tries to keep the peace (I.1.63–71). This is characteristic. Throughout the play, the 'fiery Tybalt' (I.1.109) feels resentment and anger, while, on the other hand, Benvolio tries to prevent quarrelling and fighting (for example III.1.1–4, 49–52). And, as the hero and heroine each have a cousin, so each has a close friend. Juliet's foster-mother and confidante, the Nurse, is balanced by Romeo's friend, Mercutio. Just as the old, easy-going and talkative Nurse is a contrast to the young and quiet Juliet, so the witty, intelligent and high-spirited Mercutio is a contrast to the passionate and often depressed Romeo.

The ruler of Verona, Prince Escalus, is set apart from both families, but his public commands to the two families to cease their feuding (I.1.81–103; III.1.186–97) are paralleled in their turn by Friar Laurence's secret attempts to unite Capulets and Montagues through the marriage of Romeo and Juliet (II.3.85–8). Outside each family, the Prince in public and the Friar in secret try to prevent that hostility which, in the end, kills Romeo and Juliet. The Prince as a ruler is concerned to stop 'mutiny' amongst his subjects, and the Friar, as a churchman, is also led by his office to try to stop it, but,

 CHECK THE BOOK
On adolescent rivalry and passion in the play, see Marjorie Kolb Cox, 'Adolescent Processes in *Romeo and Juliet*', *Psychoanalytical Review*, 63, 1976.

although the Prince and the Friar are outside the families, each is connected to both, and so involved in their quarrelling personally: the Prince as the kinsman of Romeo's friend Mercutio and Juliet's suitor Paris (V.3.295; III.1.109, 145, 188–9) and the Friar as father-confessor to both Romeo and Juliet (II.2.192; II.4.177–9).

And finally, all these noble figures are off-set by the servants of each household – it is, indeed, with the servants quarrelling in comic imitation of their masters that the play begins.

Clearly, the characters are not a casual collection of people, but figures brought together as part of a design, carefully arranged in contrasting groups. They are constructed not as people but as parts of a dramatic pattern. It is no accident that Shakespeare develops Mercutio and the Nurse from his source (see **Shakespeare's use of sources**): he needs them as part of his design. Though Shakespeare's characters are marvellously credible beings, realistic, it might be said, caution must be exercised in thinking about them as people. Their primary purpose is theatrical, not psychological or realistic. Their neat arrangement in pairs and as foils to each other does not reflect 'real life'; it is dramatically contrastive and thematically revealing. So Juliet's youth and innocence are made clearer by the Nurse's age and rather immoral worldly wisdom; Benvolio's peaceable nature is made plainer by Tybalt's quarrelsomeness. And Shakespeare gains dramatic effect by constantly varying the pattern: Tybalt clashes with Benvolio in I.1, but with Mercutio and Romeo in III.1. We see Juliet not only with the Nurse, but with Romeo, with Lady Capulet, with her father, with the Friar. Each time she is presented in a new light.

It is to fulfil their roles in the dramatic design that the characters each have a typical quality. Thus, the Prince is there primarily as a figure of authority and stability. He represents order – that order in society which the feud of Capulets and Montagues threatens. If we understand this, then we can see why it is fitting that it is the Prince who officially oversees the reconciliation of the families at the end of the play. His presence enforces the fact that order and harmony have been restored. A similar kind of general quality is present in all the characters: Romeo is the young lover; the Nurse the old gossip; the Friar the secret schemer whom Protestant Elizabethan England loved to imagine as typical of Roman Catholic Italy.

CONTEXT

The French composer, Charles Gounod (1818-1893), best known for his opera *Faust*, also composed an opera *Roméo et Juliette* in 1867.

This is not to say that Shakespeare does not individualise his characters. He certainly does. The following notes indicate something of their individuality, but yet they remain parts of the play, not human beings whom we can imagine meeting anywhere other than in the theatre.

ROMEO

Romeo first appears as a moody rejected lover, given to elaborate complaint about the pain caused by a love we suspect is not very deep (see **Love of Romeo and Juliet**, and **The language of love**). But he had not always been solitary and withdrawn like this. The very fact that his father, Benvolio and Mercutio all make so much of his changed 'humour' shows that his present behaviour is a drastic alteration and that he is not like the Romeo they used to know (I.1.118–57; I.4). He is well thought of in Verona. Even Capulet, the head of the rival house, admits it (I.5.65–8). He says that Romeo is 'well-governed': clearly, Romeo was not always subject to such moods. The implication is that, before he became infatuated with Rosaline, Romeo was a popular, lively and sociable member of Veronese society.

It is therefore a testimony to the truth of his feelings for Juliet that, when he has arranged his marriage to her, he is like his old self. 'Now art thou sociable. Now art thou Romeo,' exclaims Mercutio (II.4.87). Whereas the infatuation with Rosaline dulled him, Romeo's love for Juliet reveals his true liveliness. By this simple change, Shakespeare comments on the nature of the affections and, in Romeo's high spirits in II.4, shows us how witty he really is.

Once he has ceased to brood, however, Romeo is clearly rather impractical. He is all for impetuous action, but takes little consideration as to ways and means. Juliet has to point out to him that the marriage must be arranged; he is more inclined to express the rapture of his love than to plan what to do about it (II.2.139–48, 164–9). When he goes to the Friar, he is in a great hurry, but has no real suggestion to make beyond saying the Friar 'must' marry them (II.3.53–60). Later, when he meets the angry Tybalt, Romeo is at first moderate, but the death of Mercutio is too much for him: 'fire-eyed fury be my conduct now,' he cries (III.1.124) and he throws consideration to the winds.

CHECK THE BOOK
Jonathan Goldberg, ed., in his book, *Queering the Renaissance*, 1994, presents another aspect of Romeo's character, when it examines same-sex attraction and homoeroticism in the relationship between Romeo and Mercutio.

ROMEO continued

Impetuous and impractical, Romeo is also more than a little passionate, as that last example suggests. When he hears of his banishment, he behaves very much like a child, throwing himself to the ground in a frenzy of grief (III.3.65–71, 84). He has here lost all self-control. It is the Friar who brings him to himself and shows him what he now must do (III.3.109–59). It is entirely characteristic that when, in Mantua, he hears the news of Juliet's death, he reacts immediately, without waiting a moment to consider what is the best thing to do. As he rushed into marriage, collapsed into grief, so now he decides instantly to return to Verona to kill himself (V.1.24–6).

The passion and impetuosity that lurk in Romeo are his most distinctive features, and, to an extent, they are responsible for the tragedy which overwhelms the lovers. Had he been a little less hasty, less impassioned, all would have been well. A little delay in V.1 would have given time for him to learn the truth about Juliet's 'death'. On the other hand, it is this same quality which allows him to give himself so entirely and completely to Juliet. It is characteristic of Shakespeare that the same trait is at once the thing we admire and the thing we regret, both a source of strength and of fallibility.

JULIET

Juliet is a much quieter character than Romeo. She begins the play as a submissive and obedient thirteen-year-old girl who has lived a sheltered life and in the course of the play develops into a resolute woman (see **Love of Romeo and Juliet**). Romeo's character does not so much change: rather, we find out what he is really like. But Juliet does change, and the mature Juliet is a contrast to the impassioned Romeo. Her love is as deep as his, and as deeply felt (notice how she longs for the return of the Nurse at the beginning of II.5, and anticipates her wedding night in III.2). There is nothing insipid or weak about her feelings, but she has more awareness of the practicalities of the situation than Romeo and she speaks much more frankly (see **Words and truth**).

She contrasts with Romeo in another way, too. There was an element of self-deceit in Romeo's role as Rosaline's lover. Juliet, as her plain speaking shows, is above all honest, with both Romeo and herself. Because of Romeo's banishment she is reduced to playing a part, the part designed for her in the Friar's plan. But she never

CHECK THE BOOK

Marina in Shakespeare's *Pericles* is fourteen and Miranda in *The Tempest* fifteen, heroines whose youth, like Juliet's, emphasises their innocence and vulnerability.

becomes less than true to herself. Deception is not her nature, and nothing less than her love for Romeo would have prompted her to deceive her parents. That she does so is a measure not of how deceitful she is but of how independent and firm-minded she has become. She recognises only one obligation – to Romeo.

This aspect of her character is enforced by the fact that she is gradually isolated from everyone she knows and loves. This, indeed, happens to Romeo too, but he is away in Mantua throughout Act IV and it is Juliet whom we actually see struggling alone with circumstances. She is without Romeo; cut off from her parents because they do not know of her marriage; even the Nurse lets her down by suggesting bigamy when Juliet turns to her for help (III.5.213–26). Juliet is thus abandoned by everyone in the one scene, III.5, which begins with Romeo's departure. These repeated desertions are cumulatively very striking. Juliet's exclamation 'Ancient damnation!' (III.5.236) marks the final break with all the guardians of her childhood. She is now alone, a tragic heroine: 'My dismal scene I needs must act alone' (IV.3.19).

CHECK THE NET
A Web search for 'Romeo' brings up about 2.2 million sites and for 'Juliet' 1,050,000.

FRIAR LAURENCE

The Friar is the one person to whom Romeo and Juliet can both turn throughout the play. Everyone speaks well of him, and his is the voice of moderation in a stormy and violent world (see **Competing views of love, on Passion and moderation**). He is a pleasant and likeable figure, but not a very complex one. He is chiefly important as the means to promote the plot. As a character he will not sustain serious interrogation: should he have agreed to a secret marriage? should he have deceived Juliet's parents? don't his words to them in their grief when they think Juliet is dead sound like hypocrisy – he is certainly not telling the truth (IV.5.65–83)? doesn't he treat Juliet's parents cruelly, putting them through this suffering? These questions might be asked of a real friar: they cannot be asked of Friar Laurence, for there are no answers provided in the text. The Prince's verdict that he is a holy man (V.3.270) has to be accepted as a convention of the play, however much we might wonder what kind of holiness it is that can do what Friar Laurence does. In a case like this, talk of the realism of Shakespeare's characters can only mislead.

Juliet herself comes up against this difficulty. As she is about to take the potion, she raises moral questions about the Friar, that is, she treats him as a real human being with motives for his actions. She wonders whether, as he has already married her secretly to Romeo, he has actually given her poison to take so that she will die and no-one will know what he has done. This suspicion might well be entertained of a real friar who had acted like Friar Laurence. But Juliet puts aside the worry with the rather unconvincing reflection that he must be a holy man:

> What if it be a poison which the Friar
> Subtly hath ministered to have me dead,
> Lest in this marriage he should be dishonoured
> Because he married me before to Romeo?
> I fear it is. And yet methinks it should not,
> For he hath still been tried a holy man. (IV.3.24–9)

Juliet here uses almost the same words as the Prince in the last scene of the play, reasserting the type that the Friar represents. At this moment in this early play a tendency towards greater psychological complexity can be discerned: the Friar has been used as a plot device, but the character of Juliet, though the type of the innocent heroine, has developed a richer inner life which leads her to think about the Friar as an actual person might. This results in a tension between a believable being, who asks questions, and a type figure whose behaviour is determined not by psychological **verisimilitude** but by the demands of his role.

MERCUTIO

Mercutio is important in the play as a foil to Romeo and as a source of comedy, but, much more fully developed than the Friar, he is also a winning personality in himself.

CONTEXT

The eighteenth-century writer, Samuel Johnson, believed that 'Mercutio's wit, gaiety and courage will always procure him friends that wish him a longer life'.

Vivacious, lively, always talking, jesting even in death (III.1.96–9), he is a clear contrast to Romeo, but his is an independent mind such that he wins our attention in his own right. He offers us an attitude to love worth considering (see **Competing views of love, on Spiritual and sexual love**) and, although always witty, his wit is not empty. Mercutio always has a point to make. The thrust of a good many of his jokes against Romeo early in the play wins assent, and his caustic comments on Italian duels and fashionable courtiers mark him out as one whose repartee is based on acute observation (II.4.19–35). Even so, his intelligence and shrewdness do not prevent him from being killed. It was noted earlier that Shakespeare brings Mercutio into the duel in III.1 in order to show Romeo's unwillingness to fight (see **Themes, on The feud**), but this incident also shows Mercutio has deep feelings, and, what is more, feelings that can be misguided. In so assiduously pursuing the feud, in feeling Romeo has 'let the side down' by refusing to fight Tybalt, Mercutio shows a false sense of honour which, **ironically**, will contribute to the death of his friend. Mercutio had seemed to turn the play into a comedy at times: it is with his death that we know this is to be a tragedy.

> **CONTEXT**
>
> The character and role of Mercutio are almost entirely Shakespeare's invention; he plays a very small part in earlier versions of the story.

THE NURSE

The Nurse is Juliet's equivalent of Romeo's Mercutio. Like Mercutio, she does not change or develop; like him, she supplies a good deal of humour; like him, she has an attitude to love which contrasts with that of the hero and heroine (see **Spiritual and sexual love**); and, like Mercutio, she is almost entirely Shakespeare's invention, being barely mentioned in the sources.

Vulgar, coarse, quite insensitive and immoral, she can be made to sound like an old witch. Her wordiness can be very infuriating. She speaks a good deal and says very little (notice how long it takes her to say how old Juliet is in I.3 and to tell Romeo what she has come for in II.4). This can sometimes seem like a deliberate wilfulness: in II.5 she seems to have little regard for Juliet's feelings as she delays giving Romeo's message. Her garrulousness is a clear contrast to Juliet's unequivocal directness. When Juliet has something to say, she says it directly (with these examples from the Nurse we might compare Juliet's speech to the Friar in IV.1.50–67).

The Nurse contrasts with Juliet in another way, too. Once she has met Romeo, Juliet knows exactly what she thinks and what she wants. The Nurse, on the other hand, changes her mind with bewildering rapidity. She seems to support Lady Capulet in her praise of Paris (I.3.79), and then helps Juliet arrange her marriage to Romeo (II.4). After Tybalt's death, she agrees when Juliet, in her astonishment, raves against Romeo as deceitful (III.2.85–90); but when Juliet recovers herself, the Nurse readily undertakes to bring Romeo to her (III.2.138–41). She warns Romeo and Juliet of the approach of Lady Capulet in III.5, and yet, at the end of that scene, she much prefers Paris to Romeo ('Romeo's a dishclout to him') and suggests Juliet should marry Paris (III.5.213–26). And although she helped to bring about the marriage to Romeo, she is quite happy to wake Juliet in IV.5 for her marriage to Paris. In short, the Nurse agrees with whatever seems to be the opinion of the moment.

CHECK THE BOOK

For a fine characterisation of the Nurse, see Samuel Taylor Coleridge's *Shakespearean Criticism*.

And yet this is not all there is to the Nurse. Certainly, sex, child rearing and old memories make up a good deal of her conversation. She is quite without refinement, but she is also without affectation. She speaks plainly of the basic things of life she knows. To dismiss her as a meddlesome old woman, however, is to be less sympathetic than Shakespeare, who has given her an obviously genuine love for Juliet (for example in I.3.60–3) and a position of trust in the Capulet household. It is sad that she lets Juliet down at the crucial time (III.5.205–43), but she can hardly be blamed for that. She is advising what seems to her, truly, to be the best course of action, and, although she does not know it, she is more than punished by losing Juliet's confidence. This is something that would hurt her deeply. Indeed, that the Nurse does not understand the depth of Juliet's love for Romeo, and so can suggest marriage to Paris, is a measure of how far Juliet has grown up. She is no longer a little girl whom the Nurse can influence; now she is a woman with a commitment beyond the Nurse's comprehension.

LORD AND LADY CAPULET

See **Competing views of love** for a discussion of their role.

BENVOLIO AND TYBALT

These simple characters, the peacemaker and the quarreller, are obvious contrasts. They behave according to type throughout the play, and have none of the liveliness or individuality of Mercutio or the Nurse. Tybalt is always angry (I.1.65–71; I.5.54–92; III.1.34–132; these are the only times he appears in the play). He believes it is up to him to keep the quarrel alive. He takes Romeo's appearance at the party as a personal insult and determines to avenge it. By contrast, Capulet and Montague, the older men, seem inclined to let the quarrel drop (for example in I.2.1–3; I.5.54–88).

Benvolio concerns us a little more, as the friend who persuades Romeo to say why he is so depressed. But thereafter he is always for peace, and rather overshadowed by Mercutio and Tybalt. He is clearly a foil to them, and so vanishes from the play after III. 1. With both Mercutio and Tybalt dead, Benvolio is no longer needed as part of the design. That Shakespeare is so willing simply to drop a character from the play, without explanation, shows that he is thinking in terms of design, in terms of the usefulness of the characters.

> **CONTEXT**
>
> Tybalt, remarked the Romantic writer, Samuel Taylor Coleridge, 'is a man abandoned to his passion'.

PARIS

Paris is not the unpleasant character we might expect the hero's rival to be, but he is very different from Romeo. Whereas Romeo is passionate and impetuous, Paris is calm and decorous. He acts as a suitor to a young lady ought to act. Against Romeo's impetuosity, he offers us the normal form of courtship. He does not steal into the lady's garden at night, nor does he visit her room secretly. He approaches her father with a proper proposal (I.2), and, when the father offers him his daughter's hand, he accepts it, even though he knows the daughter has not been asked (III.4). Indeed, it seems that Paris has never even spoken to Juliet: all his wooing has been to Capulet. (By contrast, Romeo has spoken only to Juliet, not to her father.) Thus, Paris serves to exemplify a very different kind of love from Romeo's. His proper course of courtship seems a rather pallid thing. His affection lacks passionate involvement, and, in paying scant heed to Juliet's own wishes ('That "may be" must be, love, on Thursday next' (IV.1.20)), seems to lack respect for the loved one.

But we should not be too hard on Paris. Shakespeare, clearly, could not develop Paris's love too much, or the audience would have been distracted from Romeo and would have begun to see Juliet as torn between two equally eligible young men. As it is, we see a different kind of love offered, and one which, though it may seem pale beside Romeo's, is not necessarily insincere. When Paris does meet Juliet in IV.1 he treats her with some consideration and tenderness, and his obsequies in V.2 suggest a genuine affection. And, like Romeo, he wishes to lie with Juliet in death (V.3.72–3). Furthermore, his courage in V.3, when he fights Romeo, should prevent his being dismissed as a weak and unfeeling person.

PART FOUR

CRITICAL HISTORY

TRADITIONAL CRITICISM

Eighteenth-century criticism of Shakespeare was concerned chiefly with the structure of his plays and the extent to which this did, or did not, conform to the model of Classical drama, though the early eighteenth-century poet Alexander Pope, who edited Shakespeare's works, pointedly remarked that 'To judge … of Shakespeare by Aristotle's rules, is like trying a man by the Laws of one Country, who acted under those of another'. It was in reaction to the judgmental, and often censorious, tenor of much eighteenth-century criticism that the poets and critics of the Romantic period came to champion Shakespeare's genius, imagination and passion as far more important than matters of plot and structure. These qualities were discerned in Shakespeare's poetry, and in the authenticity this gave to the feelings of his characters. For the Romantic critic and poet Samuel Taylor Coleridge they were especially in evidence in *Romeo and Juliet*. In lectures on the play he commended the variety of its language, the individuality of its characters and the power of its depiction of passionate feeling.

CONTEXT
Since the eighteenth century the word 'Romeo' has been used in English to refer to any male lover or seducer of women.

This line in criticism culminated in A. C. Bradley's immensely influential *Shakespearean Tragedy* (1904), which treated Shakespeare's characters not as parts of a dramatic design but as living persons, each with a personal history and a fully developed psychology which could be analysed. He interpreted the action of the tragedies (though his book did not include a chapter on *Romeo and Juliet*) in terms of the personality and choices of their tragic heroes. This approach was famously mocked in an essay entitled 'How many children had Lady Macbeth?' by L. C. Knights (1933).

DECONSTRUCTION AND HISTORICISM

Following Knights, recent criticism has lost interest in characterisation. Contemporary studies are concerned much more, first, with the complexity of texts and the way that their apparent meanings are contradicted and problematised. This deconstructive approach seeks to bring out the tensions within texts and to challenge the claim that texts have a single meaning, which is what their authors intended them to mean. It is exemplified in the essays collected in John Drakakis's aptly entitled *Alternative Shakespeares* (1985).

Secondly, critics have been interested in the ways texts are shaped not by their author's intentions but by the societies and cultures which produced them, and in the extent to which they either reinforce, or work against, the political and social power systems of their time. New historicists tend to argue that the *status quo* is confirmed by textual representations of power while cultural materialists (often of a Marxist persuasion) such as Jonathan Dollimore look out for passages of resistance to institutional authority. Both are interested in how far the subversive tendencies of texts are contained. Such an approach would seek to establish how far the re-establishment of traditional order at the end of *Romeo and Juliet* closes down the challenge to that order posed by the actions of the lovers.

 CHECK THE BOOK

For a radical reading of *Romeo and Juliet* as an attack on the way human relations are constrained by social and sexual stereotypes and structures of power, see Kiernan Ryan's study entitled, simply, *Shakespeare*.

The reading offered in the Critical Approaches in these Notes has explored the ways in which the love of Romeo and Juliet is vindicated. However, approaches of a deconstructive and historicist caste might challenge that, on the grounds of what the play does not mention and what the audience might be expected to have brought to it. An uncomfortable silence is maintained about one conspicuous feature of the plot, namely, the suicide of Romeo and Juliet. The silence is uncomfortable because everyone in the Elizabethan audience would have known that suicide is a mortal sin, that there could be no burial in consecrated ground for suicides and that they had lost all hope of salvation. The play is silent on this because, of course, to introduce the notion that Romeo and Juliet are damned would run entirely against its celebration of their love. In fact, however, its silence only alerts us to the omission, for the fact would have been so glaringly obvious as to be inescapable. It is all but inconceivable that, at the end of the play, neither the Friar nor the Prince should mention it. This tension between the play's text and its cultural context problematises it in other ways: Romeo and Juliet are passionate lovers, utterly immoderate in their obsession with each other, quite incapable of compromise (as the Friar reminds us). It is this, as much as any external force, which brings them to their deaths; it is this which presents suicide to them as the only possible course. The Christian tradition and the Classical tradition, taken up by the Elizabethan world, valued restraint, moderation and reasonableness very highly. It regarded surrender to one's passion as a surrender of the capacity to make rational choices; it was to be driven by wilful desire, and so to act sinfully. Although this theme is much less pronounced in Shakespeare's play than in his sources (see **Shakespeare's use of sources**), it nevertheless cannot be written out of the story so completely as the text would wish. There is justice in their deaths since Romeo and Juliet bring their fate upon themselves through their worship of each other to the exclusion of all other moral obligations. The play retains the profile of an admonitory tale.

THE FEMINIST APPROACH

CONTEXT

For other daughters who defy their fathers with tragic consequences see Desdemona in *Othello* and Cordelia in *King Lear*.

A third strand in contemporary criticism is that of feminism. This is interested in the depiction of women, in the predominance of the male voice and gaze, in the structuring of texts by patriarchal assumptions, and in the ways in which notions of woman's inferior place are (or are not) reproduced. This approach would be interested in Capulet's assumption of the right to dispose of his daughter to another man, in Juliet's initial submission to her father's patriarchal authority (mirrored in the state by the authority exercised over his subjects by the Prince) and in her later repudiation of it. It can suggest (as does Cedric Watts in his study of the play) that the championing of the lovers in *Romeo and Juliet* issues a challenge to traditional notions of familial duty, gender relations and the character and status of women, but it could also argue that the structure of the play insists that Juliet's insubordination is punished. Everyone at the end may be chastened, but Juliet does not get away with her rebellion. Feminist critics would also ask how far the Nurse is a liberated figure, refreshingly free from inhibitions about sex, and how far trapped in a marginal role as a woman whose usefulness really ceased when she could no longer breastfeed Juliet. However, though the Nurse might seem trapped in a world of smutty jokes and garrulity, Juliet exhibits a determination, resolution and circumspection rather beyond Romeo. It is she, rather than he, who is in charge. On the other hand, it is her love for a man (and not her friendship with the Nurse) which gives her this strength.

These various contemporary approaches characteristically think of themselves as radical and committed to a left-of-centre politics; they believe that traditional readings of Shakespeare have been contrived (or 'fabricated', they are fond of saying) to support conservative thinking, traditionalism and the politics of the right. They believe that Shakespeare has been appropriated to serve the *status quo* (Prince Charles's publicly stated admiration for him might be cited). As Kiernan Ryan puts it in his lucid summary of these approaches in the opening chapter of his *Shakespeare*, 'The problem is that so far the battle for the Bard has invariably been won by forces intent on fabricating from his life and art a powerful apology for leaving the world the way it is'. The belligerent imagery here (criticism becomes a 'battle') suggests self-interest in traditional criticism, if not a deliberate plot; it is equated with 'forces intent' on resisting political change. One might remark that criticism such as Ryan's is still less impartial, his political commitment still more overt; but to this the reply would be that all criticism is political.

CHECK THE BOOK

On the significance of characters' names in *Romeo and Juliet*, see Murray J. Levith, *What's in Shakespeare's Names*, 1978.

PART FIVE

BACKGROUND

WILLIAM SHAKESPEARE'S LIFE

There are no personal records of Shakespeare's life. Official documents and occasional references to him by contemporary dramatists enable us to draw the main outline of his public life, but his private life remains hidden. Although not at all unusual for a writer of his time, this lack of first-hand evidence has tempted many to read his plays as personal records and to look in them for clues to his character and convictions. The results are unconvincing, partly because Renaissance art was not subjective or designed primarily to express its creator's personality, and partly because the drama of any period is very difficult to read biographically. Except when plays are written by committed dramatists to promote social or political causes (as by Shaw or Brecht), it is all but impossible to decide who amongst the variety of fictional characters in a drama represents the dramatist, or which of the various and often conflicting points of view expressed is authorial.

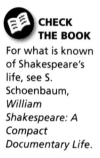

CHECK THE BOOK

For what is known of Shakespeare's life, see S. Schoenbaum, *William Shakespeare: A Compact Documentary Life*.

What we do know can be quickly summarised. Shakespeare was born into a well-to-do family in the market town of Stratford-upon-Avon in Warwickshire, where he was baptised, in Holy Trinity Church, on 26 April 1564. His father, John Shakespeare, was a prosperous glover and leather merchant who became a person of some importance in the town: in 1565 he was elected an alderman, and in 1568 he became high bailiff (or mayor) of Stratford. In 1557 he had married Mary Arden. Their third child (of eight) and eldest son, William, learned to read and write at the primary (or 'petty') school in Stratford and then, it seems probable, attended the local grammar school, where he would have studied Latin, history, logic and rhetoric. In November 1582 William, then aged eighteen, married Anne Hathaway, who was twenty-six years old. They had a daughter, Susanna, in May 1583, and twins, Hamnet and Judith, in 1585.

Shakespeare next appears in the historical record in 1592 when he was mentioned as a London actor and playwright in a pamphlet by the dramatist Robert Greene. These 'lost years' 1585–92 have been the subject of much speculation, but how they were occupied remains as much a mystery as when Shakespeare left Stratford, and why. In his pamphlet, *Greene's Groatsworth of Wit*, Greene expresses to his fellow dramatists his outrage that the 'upstart crow' Shakespeare has the impudence to believe he 'is as well able to bombast out a blank verse as the best of you'. To have aroused this hostility from a rival, Shakespeare must, by 1592, have been long enough in London to have made a name for himself as a playwright. We may conjecture that he had left Stratford in 1586 or 1587.

During the next twenty years, Shakespeare continued to live in London, regularly visiting his wife and family in Stratford. He continued to act, but his chief fame was as a dramatist. From 1594 he wrote exclusively for the Lord Chamberlain's Men, which rapidly became the leading dramatic company and from 1603 enjoyed the patronage of James I as the King's Men. His plays were extremely popular and he became a shareholder in his theatre company. He was able to buy lands around Stratford and a large house in the town, to which he retired about 1611. He died there on 23 April 1616 and was buried in Holy Trinity Church on 25 April.

SHAKESPEARE'S DRAMATIC CAREER

Between the late 1580s and 1613 Shakespeare wrote thirty-seven plays, and contributed to some by other dramatists. This was by no means an exceptional number for a professional playwright of the times. The exact date of the composition of individual plays is a matter of debate – for only a few plays is the date of their first performance known – but the broad outlines of Shakespeare's dramatic career have been established. He began in the late 1580s and early 1590s by rewriting earlier plays and working with plotlines inspired by the Classics. He concentrated on comedies (such as *The Comedy of Errors*, 1590–4, which derived from the Latin playwright Plautus) and plays dealing with English history (such as the three parts of *Henry VI*, 1589–92), though he also tried his hand at bloodthirsty revenge tragedy (*Titus Andronicus*, 1592–3, indebted to both Ovid and Seneca). During the 1590s Shakespeare developed his expertise in these kinds of play to write such comic masterpieces such as *A Midsummer Night's Dream* (1594–5) and *As*

WWW. CHECK THE NET

For information of Shakespeare's home town Stratford-upon-Avon, including sites associated with the dramatist, visit http://www. stratford.co.uk

You Like It (1599–1600) and history plays such as Henry IV
(1596–8) and Henry V (1598–9).

As the new century begins a new note is detectable. Plays such as
Troilus and Cressida (1601–2) and Measure for Measure (1603–4),
poised between comedy and tragedy, evoke complex responses.
Because of their generic uncertainty and ambivalent tone such
works are sometimes referred to as 'problem plays', but it is tragedy
which comes to dominate the extraordinary sequence of
masterpieces: Hamlet (1600–1), Othello (1602–4), King Lear
(1605–6), Macbeth (1605–6) and Antony and Cleopatra (1606).

In the last years of his dramatic career, Shakespeare wrote a group
of plays of a quite different kind. These 'romances', as they are often
called, are in many ways the most remarkable of all his plays. The
group comprises Pericles (1608), Cymbeline (1609–11), The Winter's
Tale (1610–11) and The Tempest (1610–11). These plays
(particularly Cymbeline) reprise many of the situations and themes
of the earlier dramas but in fantastical and exotic dramatic designs
which, set in distant lands, covering large tracts of time and
involving music, mime, dance and tableaux, have something of the
qualities of masques and pageants. The situations which in the
tragedies had led to disaster are here resolved: the great theme is
restoration and reconciliation. Where in the tragedies Ophelia,
Desdemona and Cordelia died, the daughters of these plays –
Marina, Imogen, Perdita, Miranda – survive and are reunited with
their parents and lovers.

THE TEXTS OF SHAKESPEARE'S PLAYS

Nineteen of Shakespeare's plays were printed during his lifetime in
what are called '**quartos**' (books, each containing one play, and made
up of sheets of paper each folded twice to make four leaves).
Shakespeare, however, did not supervise their publication. This was
not unusual. When a playwright had sold a play to a dramatic
company he sold his rights in it: copyright belonged to whoever had
possession of an actual copy of the text, and so consequently authors
had no control over what happened to their work. Anyone who
could get hold of the text of a play might publish it if they wished.

Hence, what found its way into print might be the author's copy, but it might be an actor's copy or prompt copy, perhaps cut or altered for performance; sometimes, actors (or even members of the audience) might publish what they could remember of the text. Printers, working without the benefit of the author's oversight, introduced their own errors, through misreading the manuscript for example, and by 'correcting' what seemed to them not to make sense.

In 1623 John Heminges and Henry Condell, two actors in Shakespeare's company, collected together texts of thirty-six of Shakespeare's plays (*Pericles* was omitted) and published them in a large **folio** (a book in which each sheet of paper is folded once in half, to give two leaves). This, the First Folio, was followed by later editions in 1632, 1663 and 1685. Despite its appearance of authority, however, the texts in the First Folio still present many difficulties, for there are printing errors and confused passages in the plays, and its texts often differ significantly from those of the earlier quartos, when these exist.

Shakespeare's texts have, then, been through a number of inter-mediaries. We do not have his authority for any one of his plays, and hence we cannot know exactly what it was that he wrote. Bibliographers, textual critics and editors have spent a great deal of effort on endeavouring to get behind the errors, uncertainties and contradictions in the available texts to recover the plays as Shakespeare originally wrote them. What we read is the result of these efforts. Modern texts are what editors have constructed from the available evidence: they correspond to no sixteenth- or seventeenth-century editions, and to no early performance of a Shakespeare play. Furthermore, these composite texts differ from each other, for different editors read the early texts differently and come to different conclusions. A Shakespeare text is an unstable and a contrived thing.

Often, of course, its judgements embody, if not the personal prejudices of the editor, then the cultural preferences of the time in which he or she was working. Growing awareness of this has led recent scholars to distrust the whole editorial enterprise and to repudiate the attempt to construct a 'perfect' text. Stanley Wells and Gary Taylor, the editors of the Oxford edition of *The Complete*

CHECK THE NET
http://shakespeare.palomar.edu/ attempts to provide a complete guide to scholarly materials on Shakespeare on the Web.

Works (1988), point out that almost certainly the texts of Shakespeare's plays were altered in performance, and from one performance to another, so that there may never have been a single version. They note, too, that Shakespeare probably revised and rewrote some plays. They do not claim to print a definitive text of any play, but prefer what seems to them the 'more theatrical' version, and when there is a great difference between available versions, as with *King Lear*, they print two texts.

SHAKESPEARE AND THE ENGLISH RENAISSANCE

Shakespeare arrived in London at the very time that the Elizabethan period was poised to become the 'golden age' of English literature. Although Elizabeth reigned as queen from 1558 to 1603, the term 'Elizabethan' is used very loosely in a literary sense to refer to the period 1580 to 1625, when the great works of the age were produced. (Sometimes the later part of this period is distinguished as 'Jacobean', from the Latin form of James – James I of England and VI of Scotland reigned from 1603 to 1625.) The poet Edmund Spenser heralded this new age with his pastoral poem *The Shepheardes Calender* (1579) and in his essay *An Apologie for Poetrie* (written about 1580, although not published until 1595) his friend Sir Philip Sidney championed the imaginative power of the 'speaking picture of poesy', famously declaring that 'Nature never set forth the earth in so rich a tapestry as divers poets have done … Her world is brazen, the poets only deliver a golden'.

Spenser and Sidney were part of that rejuvenating movement in European culture which since the nineteenth century has been known by the term *Renaissance*. Meaning literally *rebirth* it denotes a revival and redirection of artistic and intellectual endeavour which began in Italy in the fourteenth century in the poetry of **Petrarch**. It spread gradually northwards across Europe, and is first detectable in England in the early sixteenth century in the writings of the scholar and statesman Sir Thomas More and in the poetry of Sir Thomas Wyatt and Henry Howard, Earl of Surrey. Its keynote was a curiosity in thought which challenged old assumptions and traditions. To the innovative spirit of the Renaissance, the preceding ages appeared dully unoriginal and conformist.

CONTEXT

By his contemporaries Sir Philip Sidney (1554-86), courtier, diplomat, writer and soldier, was taken to embody the Renaissance ideal of the complete gentleman.

That spirit was fuelled by the rediscovery of many Classical texts and the culture of Greece and Rome. This fostered a confidence in human reason and in human potential which, in every sphere, challenged old convictions. The discovery of America and its peoples (Columbus had sailed in 1492) demonstrated that the world was a larger and stranger place than had been thought. The cosmological speculation of Copernicus (later confirmed by Galileo) that the sun, not the earth, was the centre of our planetary system challenged the centuries-old belief that the earth and human beings were at the centre of the cosmos. The pragmatic political philosophy of Machiavelli seemed to cut politics free from its traditional link with morality by permitting to statesmen any means which secured the desired end. And the religious movements we know collectively as the Reformation broke with the Church of Rome and set the individual conscience, not ecclesiastical authority, at the centre of the religious life. Nothing, it seemed, was beyond questioning, nothing impossible.

> **CONTEXT**
>
> *The Prince* (1513), a work of political theory by the Florentine statesman Niccolò Machiavelli (1469–1527), was popularly supposed in England to sanction the adoption of any means, no matter how vicious, to achieve a political end.

Shakespeare's drama is innovative and challenging in exactly the way of the Renaissance. It questions the beliefs, assumptions and politics upon which Elizabethan society was founded. And although the plays always conclude in a restoration of order and stability, many critics are inclined to argue that their imaginative energy goes into subverting, rather than reinforcing, traditional values. They would point out that the famous speech on hierarchical order in *Troilus and Cressida* (I.3.86–124) or Katerina's speech on wifely submission to patriarchal authority in *The Taming of the Shrew* (V.2.146–60) appear to be rendered **ironic** by the action of the plays in which they occur. Convention, audience expectation and censorship all required the *status quo* to be endorsed by the plots' conclusions, but the dramas find ways to allow alternative sentiments to be expressed. Frequently, figures of authority are undercut by some comic or **parodic** figure: against the Duke in *Measure for Measure* is set Lucio; against Prospero in *The Tempest*, Caliban; against Henry IV, Falstaff. Despairing, critical, dissident, disillusioned, unbalanced, rebellious, mocking voices are repeatedly to be heard in the plays, rejecting, resenting, defying the established order. They belong always to marginal, socially unacceptable figures, 'licensed', as it were, by their situations to say what would be unacceptable from socially privileged or responsible citizens. The question is: are such characters given these views to discredit them, or were they the only ones through whom a voice could be given to radical and dissident ideas? Is Shakespeare a conservative or a revolutionary?

Renaissance culture was intensely nationalistic. With the break-up of the internationalism of the Middle Ages the evolving nation states which still mark the map of Europe began for the first time to acquire distinctive cultural identities. There was intense rivalry among them as they sought to achieve in their own vernacular languages a culture which could equal that of Greece and Rome. Spenser's great allegorical epic poem *The Faerie Queene*, which began to appear from 1590, celebrated Elizabeth and was intended to outdo the poetic achievements of France and Italy and to stand beside the works of Virgil and Homer. Shakespeare is equally preoccupied with national identity. His history plays tell an epic story which examines how modern England came into being through the conflicts of the fifteenth-century Wars of the Roses which brought the Tudors to the throne. He is fascinated, too, by the related subject of politics and the exercise of power. With the collapse of medieval feudalism and the authority of local barons, the royal court in the Renaissance came to assume a new status as the centre of power and patronage. It was here that the destiny of a country was shaped. Courts, and how to succeed in them, consequently fascinated the Renaissance; and they fascinated Shakespeare and his audience.

That is why we are usually at court in his plays, and in the company of courtiers. But the dramatic gaze is not merely admiring; through a variety of devices, a critical perspective is brought to bear. The court may be paralleled by a very different world, revealing uncomfortable similarities (for example, Henry's court and the Boar's Head tavern, ruled over by Falstaff in *Henry IV*). Its hypocrisy may be bitterly denounced (for example, in the diatribes of the mad Lear) and its self-seeking ambition represented disturbingly in the figure of a Machiavellian villain (such as Edmund in *Lear*) or a malcontent (such as Iago in *Othello*). Shakespeare is fond of displacing the court to another context, the better to examine its assumptions and pretensions and to offer alternatives to the courtly life (for example, in the pastoral setting of the forest of Arden in *As You Like It* or Prospero's island in *The Tempest*).

Courtiers are frequently figures of fun whose unmanly sophistication ('neat and trimly dressed, / Fresh as a bridegroom ... perfumed like a milliner', says Hotspur of such a man in *Henry IV*, I.3.33–6) is contrasted with plain-speaking integrity: Oswald is set against Kent in *King Lear*.

(When thinking of these matters, we should remember that stage plays were subject to censorship, and any criticism had therefore to be muted or oblique: direct criticism of the monarch or contemporary English court would not be tolerated. This has something to do with why Shakespeare's plays are always set either in the past, or abroad.)

The nationalism of the English Renaissance was reinforced by Protestantism. Henry VIII had broken with Rome in the 1530s and in Shakespeare's time there was an independent Protestant state church. Because the Pope in Rome had excommunicated Queen Elizabeth as a heretic and relieved the English of their allegiance to the Crown, there was deep suspicion of Roman Catholics as potential traitors. This was enforced by the attempted invasion of the Spanish Armada in 1588. This was a religiously inspired crusade to overthrow Elizabeth and restore England to Roman Catholic allegiance. Roman Catholicism was hence easily identified with hostility to England. Its association with disloyalty and treachery was enforced by the Gunpowder Plot of 1605, a Roman Catholic attempt to destroy the government of England.

> **CONTEXT**
>
> The attempt of Guy Fawkes and his fellow Roman Catholic conspirators to blow up the House of Commons in 1605 is still commemorated by the traditional bonfires of Guy Fawkes' Night on 5 November.

Shakespeare's plays are remarkably free from direct religious sentiment, but their emphases are Protestant. Young women, for example, are destined for marriage, not for nunneries (precisely what Isabella appears to escape at the end of *Measure for Measure*); friars are dubious characters, full of schemes and deceptions, if with benign intentions, as in *Much Ado About Nothing* or *Romeo and Juliet*. (We should add, though, that Puritans, extreme Protestants, are even less kindly treated: think of Malvolio in *Twelfth Night*!) The central figures of the plays are frequently individuals beset by temptation, by the lure of evil – Angelo in *Measure for Measure*, Othello, Lear, Macbeth – and not only in tragedies: Falstaff is described as 'that old white-bearded Satan' (*1 Henry IV*, II.4.454). We follow their inner struggles. Shakespeare's heroes have the preoccupation with self and the introspective tendencies encouraged by Protestantism: his tragic heroes are haunted by their consciences, seeking their true selves, agonising over what course of action to take as they follow what can often be understood as a kind of spiritual progress towards heaven or hell.

SHAKESPEARE'S THEATRE

The theatre for which the plays were written was one of the most remarkable innovations of the Renaissance. There had been no theatres or acting companies during the medieval period. Performed on carts and in open spaces at Christian festivals, plays had been almost exclusively religious. Such professional actors as there were wandered the country putting on a variety of entertainments in the yards of inns, on makeshift stages in market squares, or anywhere else suitable. They did not perform full-length plays, but mimes, juggling and comedy acts. Such actors were regarded by officialdom and polite society as little better than vagabonds and layabouts.

 CHECK THE FILM
The Elizabethan world of competing London theatre companies and impoverished actors is vigorously brought to the screen in John Madden's 1998 film, *Shakespeare in Love*.

Just before Shakespeare went to London all this began to change. A number of young men who had been to the universities of Oxford and Cambridge came to London in the 1580s and began to write plays which made use of what they had learned about the Classical drama of ancient Greece and Rome. Plays such as Lyly's *Alexander, Campaspe and Diogenes* (1584), Marlowe's *Tamburlaine the Great* (about 1587) and Thomas Kyd's *The Spanish Tragedy* (1588–9) were unlike anything that had been written in English before. They were full-length plays on secular subjects, taking their plots from history and legend, adopting many of the devices of Classical drama, and offering a range of characterisation and situation hitherto unattempted in English drama. With the exception of Lyly's prose dramas, they were in **blank verse** (unrhymed iambic pentameters) which the Earl of Surrey had introduced into English earlier in the sixteenth century. This was a freer and more expressive medium than the rhymed verse of medieval drama. It was the drama of these 'university wits' which Shakespeare challenged when he came to London. Greene was one of them, and we have heard how little he liked this Shakespeare setting himself up as a dramatist.

The most significant change of all, however, was that these dramatists wrote for the professional theatre. In 1576 James Burbage built the first permanent theatre in England, in Shoreditch, just beyond London's northern boundary. It was called simply 'The Theatre'. Others soon followed. Thus, when Shakespeare came to London, there was a flourishing drama, theatres and companies of actors waiting for him, such as there had never been before in England. His company performed at James Burbage's Theatre until 1596, and used the Swan and Curtain until they moved into their own new theatre, the Globe, in 1599. (The Globe was burned down in 1613 when a cannon was fired during a performance of Shakespeare's *Henry VIII*.) We know that *Romeo and Juliet* was played at the Curtain, and, as a popular play, it would have been presented at the Globe as well.

With the completion in 1996 of Sam Wanamaker's project to construct in London a replica of The Globe, and with productions now running there, a version of Shakespeare's theatre can be experienced at first hand. It is very different to the usual modern experience of drama. The form of the Elizabethan theatre derived from the inn yards and animal baiting rings in which actors had been accustomed to perform in the past. They were circular wooden buildings with a paved courtyard in the middle open to the sky. A rectangular stage jutted out into the middle of this yard. Some of the audience stood in the yard (or 'pit') to watch the play. They were thus on three sides of the stage, close up to it and on a level with it. These 'groundlings' paid only a penny to get in, but for wealthier spectators there were seats in three covered tiers or galleries between the inner and outer walls of the building, extending round most of the auditorium and overlooking the pit and the stage. Such a theatre could hold about 3,000 spectators. The yards were just over 24 m. in diameter and the rectangular stage approximately 12 × 9 m. and 1.67 m high. Shakespeare aptly called such a theatre a 'wooden O' in the Prologue to *Henry V* (line 13).

The stage itself was partially covered by a roof or canopy which projected from the wall at the rear of the stage and was supported by two posts at the front. This protected the stage and performers from inclement weather, and to it were secured winches and other machinery for stage effects. On either side at the back of the stage

www. CHECK THE NET

For information about the London reconstruction of Shakespeare's Globe, visit **http://www. shakespeares- globe.org/**.

THE GLOBE THEATRE,

On the Bankside.

As it appeared in the reign of King James I.

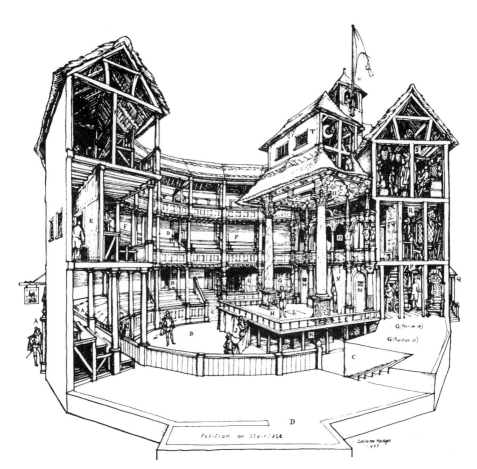

A CONJECTURAL RECONSTRUCTION OF THE INTERIOR OF THE GLOBE PLAYHOUSE

AA	Main entrance	N	Curtained 'place behind the stage'
B	The Yard	O	Gallery above the stage, used as required
CC	Entrances to lowest galleries		sometimes by musicians, sometimes by
D	Entrance to staircase and upper galleries		spectators, and often as part of the play
E	Corridor serving the different sections of the	P	Back-stage area (the tiring-house)
	middle gallery	Q	Tiring-house door
F	Middle gallery ('Twopenny Rooms')	R	Dressing-rooms
G	'Gentlemen's Rooms or Lords Rooms'	S	Wardrobe and storage
H	The stage	T	The hut housing the machine for lowering
J	The hanging being put up round the stage		enthroned gods, etc., to the stage
K	The 'Hell' under the stage	U	The 'Heavens'
L	The stage trap, leading down to the Hell	W	Hoisting the playhouse flag
MM	Stage doors		

was a door. These led into the dressing room (or 'tiring house') and it was by means of these doors that actors entered and left the stage. Between these doors was a small recess or alcove which was curtained off. Such a 'discovery place' served, for example, for Juliet's bedroom when in Act IV Scene 4 of *Romeo and Juliet* the Nurse went to the back of the stage and drew the curtain to find, or 'discover' in Elizabethan English, Juliet apparently dead on her bed. Above the discovery place was a balcony, used for the famous balcony scenes of *Romeo and Juliet* (II.2 and III.5), or for the battlements of Richard's castle when he is confronted by Bolingbroke in *Richard II* (III.3). Actors (all parts in the Elizabethan theatre were taken by boys or men) had access to the area beneath the stage; from here, in the 'cellarage', would have come the voice of the ghost of Hamlet's father (*Hamlet*, II.1.150–82).

On these stages there was very little in the way of scenery or props – there was nowhere to store them (there were no wings in this theatre) nor any way to set them up (no tabs across the stage), and, anyway, productions had to be transportable for performance at court or at noble houses. The stage was bare, which is why characters often tell us where they are: there was nothing on the stage to indicate location. It is also why location is so rarely topographical, and much more often symbolic. It suggests a dramatic mood or situation, rather than a place: Lear's barren heath reflects his destitute state, as the storm his emotional turmoil.

 CHECK THE NET

For information about the Royal Shakespeare Company, one of the finest theatre companies in the world, based in Stratford-upon-Avon, visit http://www.rsc.org.uk.

None of the plays printed in Shakespeare's lifetime marks Act or scene divisions. These have been introduced by later editors, but they should not mislead us into supposing that there was any break in Elizabethan performances such as might happen today while the curtains are closed and the set is changed. The staging of Elizabethan plays was continuous, with the many short 'scenes' of which Shakespeare's plays are often constructed following one after another in quick succession. We have to think of a more fluid, and much faster, production than we are generally used to: in the prologues to *Romeo and Juliet* (line 12) and *Henry VIII* (line 13) Shakespeare speaks of only two hours as the playing time.

We can see the kind of thing that happened from the stage directions in *Romeo and Juliet*. In I.4, Romeo and his friends decide to go to Capulet's party. At the end of the scene they '*march about the stage*' while the serving-men come on to begin I.5. This represents their going into Capulet's house: there would have been no break in the actual performance. Again, in II.1, Mercutio and Benvolio are looking for Romeo. Failing to find him, they leave, and '*coming forward*' he begins II.2. His first line actually makes a rhyming verse *couplet* with Benvolio's last line of II.1. Clearly, although the scene of the action has changed (Mercutio and Benvolio are outside Capulet's garden; Romeo is inside it), there is no break in the play. Romeo comes straight on. A different kind of example occurs in III.5. This begins '*aloft*', as the stage direction puts it, that is, on the balcony at the rear of the stage. When Romeo has left by climbing down to the stage, which here represents the garden (III.5.42), Juliet comes down by the stairs to the tiring house and enters the stage through one of the rear doors to meet her mother in the house (III.5.64–5). In this scene, then, the stage has represented two different places (the garden and the interior of the house) but the acting goes on regardless.

It is because of this continuous staging and the lack of scenery that characters in Shakespeare's plays often tell the audience what locality the stage represents at different moments. Romeo's last words in II.2, for example, set the scene for II.3. Similarly, Romeo's words at II.2.107–8 create the scene in the imagination of the audience. On the other hand, we often cannot tell where a scene is set. There is no evidence in the text, for example, for the locality of I.2 or II.4 of *Romeo and Juliet*. Modern editors often supply a locale for such scenes, but it can be safely assumed that if Shakespeare's characters do not say where they are, then their location does not matter much. The lack of a curtain across the stage in the Elizabethan theatre explains why scenes often end with rhyming lines. These show the audience that the scene has ended, and prepare them for a new scene (for example, the final two lines of V. 1 in *Romeo and Juliet*). And because actors were in full view from the moment they set foot on the stage, entrances and exits had to be written in as part of the play. Characters speak as they enter or leave the stage because otherwise there would have been a silence while, in full view, they took up their positions (for example, in *Romeo*

CHECK THE NET

http://www. shakespeare-country.co.uk/ is the official tourist site for Shakespeare's home town and county.

and Juliet, I.3.1–5; I.4.113–4; I.5.144). For the same reason, dead bodies had always to be removed by the actors in the course of the play: they cannot get up and walk off (so Mercutio goes off-stage to die and Tybalt's body is carried off, III. 1.108, 196).

In 1608 Shakespeare's company, the King's Men, acquired the Blackfriars Theatre, a smaller, rectangular indoor theatre, holding about 700 people, with seats for all the members of the audience, facilities for elaborate stage effects and, because it was enclosed, artificial lighting. It has been suggested that the plays written for this 'private' theatre differed from those written for the Globe, since, as it cost more to go to a private theatre, the audience came from a higher social stratum and demanded the more elaborate and courtly entertainment which Shakespeare's romances provide. However, the King's Men continued to play in the Globe in the summer, using Blackfriars in the winter, and it is not certain that Shakespeare's last plays were written specifically for the Blackfriars Theatre, or first performed there.

READING SHAKESPEARE

Shakespeare's plays were written for this stage, but there is also a sense in which they were written *by* this stage. The material and physical circumstances of their production in such theatres had a profound effect upon the nature of Elizabethan plays. Unless we bear this in mind, we are likely to find them very strange, for we will read with expectations shaped by our own familiarity with modern fiction and modern drama. This is, by and large, realistic; it seeks to persuade us that what we are reading or watching is really happening. This is quite foreign to Shakespeare. If we try to read him like this, we shall find ourselves irritated by the improbabilities of his plot, confused by his chronology, puzzled by locations, frustrated by unanswered questions and dissatisfied by the motivation of the action. The absurd ease with which disguised persons pass through Shakespeare's plays is a case in point: why does no-one recognise people they know so well? There is a great deal of psychological accuracy in Shakespeare's plays, but we are far from any attempt at realism.

CONTEXT

In 1680 the playwright Thomas Otway adapted the plot of *Romeo and Juliet* to an ancient Roman setting in his play, *The History and Fall of Caius Marius*.

The reason is that in Shakespeare's theatre it was impossible to pretend that the audience was not watching a contrived performance. In a modern theatre, the audience is encouraged to forget itself as it becomes absorbed by the action on stage. The worlds of the spectators and of the actors are sharply distinguished by the lighting: in the dark auditorium the audience is passive, silent, anonymous, receptive and attentive; on the lighted stage the actors are active, vocal, demonstrative and dramatic. (The distinction is, of course, still more marked in the cinema.) There is no communication between the two worlds: for the audience to speak would be interruptive; for the actors to address the audience would be to break the illusion of the play. In the Elizabethan theatre, this distinction did not exist, and for two reasons: first, performances took place in the open air and in daylight which illuminated everyone equally; secondly, the spectators were all around the stage (and wealthier spectators actually on it), and were dressed no differently to the actors, who wore contemporary dress. In such a theatre, spectators would be as aware of each other as of the actors; they could not lose their identity in a corporate group, nor could they ever forget that they were spectators at a performance. There was no chance that they could believe 'this is really happening'.

This, then, was communal theatre, not only in the sense that it was going on in the middle of a crowd but in the sense that the crowd joined in. Elizabethan audiences had none of our deference: they did not keep quiet, or arrive on time, or remain for the whole performance. They joined in, interrupted, even getting on the stage. And plays were preceded and followed by jigs and clowning. It was all much more like our experience of a pantomime, and at a pantomime we are fully aware, and are meant to be aware, that we are watching games being played with reality. The conventions of pantomime revel in their own artificiality: the Dame's monstrous false breasts signal that 'she' is a man.

Something very similar is the case with Elizabethan theatre: it utilised its very theatricality. Instead of trying to persuade spectators that they are not in a theatre watching a performance, Elizabethan plays acknowledge the presence of the audience. It is addressed not only by prologues, epilogues and choruses, but in

 CHECK THE FILM

Kenneth MacMillan's choreography to Sergei Prokofiev's 1938 ballet score of *Romeo and Juliet* was filmed in 1966 and starred Rudolph Nureyev and Margot Fonteyn.

soliloquies. There is no realistic reason why characters should suddenly explain themselves to empty rooms, but, of course, it is not an empty room. The actor is surrounded by people. Soliloquies are not addressed to the world of the play: they are for the audience's benefit. And that audience's complicity is assumed: when a character like Prospero declares himself to be invisible, it is accepted that he is. Disguises are taken to be impenetrable, however improbable, and we are to accept impossibly contrived situations, such as barely hidden characters remaining undetected (indeed, on the Elizabethan stage there was nowhere at all they could hide!).

These, then, are plays which are aware of themselves as dramas; in critical terminology, they are **self-reflexive**, commenting upon themselves as dramatic pieces and prompting the audience to think about the theatrical experience. They do this not only through their direct address to the audience but through their fondness for the play-within-a-play (which reminds the audience that the encompassing play is also a play) and their constant use of images from, and allusions to, the theatre. They are fascinated by role playing, by acting, appearance and reality. Things are rarely what they seem, either in comedy (for example, in *A Midsummer Night's Dream*) or tragedy (*Romeo and Juliet*). This offers one way to think about those disguises: they are thematic rather than realistic. Kent's disguise in *Lear* reveals his true, loyal self, while Edmund, who is not disguised, hides his true self. In *As You Like It*, Rosalind is more truly herself disguised as a man than when dressed as a woman.

CONTEXT

In 1845, in a London production of *Romeo and Juliet* two American actresses, Charlotte and Susan Cushman, took the lead roles of Romeo and Juliet, to great applause.

The effect of all this is to confuse the distinction we would make between 'real life' and 'acting'. The case of Rosalind, for example, raises searching questions about gender roles, about how far it is 'natural' to be womanly or manly: how does the stage, on which a man can play a woman playing a man (and have a man fall in love with him/her!), differ from life, in which we assume the roles we think appropriate to masculine and feminine behaviour? The same is true of political roles: when a Richard II or Lear is so aware of the regal part he is performing, of the trappings and rituals of kingship, their plays raise the uncomfortable possibility that the answer to the question, what constitutes a successful king, is simply: a good actor. Indeed, human life generally is repeatedly rendered through the imagery of the stage, from Macbeth's 'Life's but a walking shadow, a

poor player / That struts and frets his hour upon the stage / And
then is heard no more ...' (V.5.23–5) to Prospero's paralleling of
human life to a performance which, like the globe (both world and
theatre) will end (IV.I.146– 58). When life is a fiction, like this play,
or this play is a fiction like life, what is the difference? 'All the
world's a stage ...' (*As You Like It*, II.7.139).

World events

1492 Columbus sails to America

1534 Henry VIII breaks with Rome and declares himself head of the Church of England

1556 Archbishop Cranmer burnt at the stake

1558 Elizabeth I accedes to throne

Shakespeare's life

1564 (26 April) William Shakespeare baptised, Stratford-upon-Avon (birth traditionally dated 23 April, St George's Day)

Literature and the arts

1374 Death of Petrarch, most popular poet of the Italian Renaissance

1476 Masuccio Salernitano writes original tale of Romeo and Juliet

1487 Matteomaria Boiardo, *Orlando Innamorato*, the love story of Orlando and Angelica

1513 Niccolò Machiavelli, *The Prince*

1528 Castiglione, *Book of the Courtier*

1532 Ludovico Ariosto, *Orlando Furioso* continues Boiardo's love story

1562 Arthur Brooke, *The Tragicall Historye of Romeus and Juliet*. Birth of Lope de Vega, Spanish dramatist

1567 William Painter, 'The goodly Historye of the true and constant love between Rhomeo and Julietta'

World events	Shakespeare's life	Literature and the arts
1568 Mary Queen of Scots taken prisoner by Elizabeth I		
1570 Elizabeth I excommunicated by Pope Pius V		
1571 The Battle of Lepanto		
		1576 James Burbage builds the first theatre in England, at Shoreditch
1577 Francis Drake sets out on round the world voyage		
		1579 Edmund Spenser, *The Shepheardes Calender*
		1580 (c.) Sir Philip Sidney, *An Apologie for Poetrie*
1582 Outbreak of the Plague in London	**1582** He marries Anne Hathaway	
	1583 His daughter, Susanna, born	
1584 Raleigh's sailors land in Virginia		**1584** John Lyly's *Alexander, Campaspe and Diogenes*
	1585 His twins, Hamnet and Judith, born	
1587 Execution of Mary Queen of Scots after implication in plot to murder Elizabeth I	**late 1580s – early 90s** He probably *writes Henry VI (Parts I, II, III)* and *Richard III*	**1587** Christopher Marlowe, *Tamburlaine the Great*
1588 The Spanish Armada defeated		**1588-9** Thomas Kyd, *The Spanish Tragedy*
1589 Accession of Henri IV to French throne		
		1590 Edmund Spenser, *The Faerie Queene (Books I-III)*
		1591 Sir John Harington translates *Orlando Furioso* into English

World events	Shakespeare's life	Literature and the arts
1592 Plague in London closes theatres	**1592** Shakespeare recorded as being a London actor and an 'upstart crow'	**1592** Christopher Marlowe, *Dr. Faustus*
	1592-4 He writes *Comedy of Errors*	**1593** Christopher Marlowe killed in a Deptford tavern
	1594 onwards, He writes exclusively for the Lord Chamberlain's Men	**1594** Publication of Marlowe's *Dido, Queen of Carthage*
	1594 *The Comedy of Errors* first acted	
	1595 (c.) His *Two Gentlemen of Verona, The Taming of the Shrew* and *Love's Labour's Lost* are thought to have been written before this year. He writes *Romeo and Juliet* and *A Midsummer Night's Dream.*	**1595** Michel de Montaigne, *Essais*
1596 Drake perishes on expedition to West Indies		**1596** Edmund Spencer, *The Faerie Queene (Books IV–VI)*
		1598-9 Globe Theatre built at Southwark
		1598 Ben Jonson, *Every Man in his Humour*
		1599 Ben Jonson, *Every Man out of his Humour*
	1600 *A Midsummer Night's Dream, Much Ado about Nothing* and *The Merchant of Venice* printed; *Twelfth Night* probably written	**1600** Richard Hakluyt, *Principal Navigations and Voyages of the English Nation* (final version)
	1600-1 Shakespeare's *Hamlet*	
	1602 His *Troilus and Cressida* probably written	
1603 Death of Queen Elizabeth I; accession of James I (VI of Scotland)	**1603 onwards,** his company enjoys patronage of James I as the King's Men	

World events	Shakespeare's life	Literature and the arts
	1604 His *Othello* performed	
1605 Discovery of Guy Fawkes's plot to blow up the Houses of Parliament	**1605** First version of his *King Lear*	**1605** Cervantes, *Don Quijote de la Mancha*
		1605 Francis Bacon, *The Advancement of Learning*
	1606 He writes *Macbeth*	**1606** Ben Jonson, *Volpone*; Michael Drayton, *Odes*
	1606-7 He probably writes *Antony and Cleopatra*	
	1608 The King's Men acquire Blackfriars Theatre for winter performances	
1609 Galileo constructs first astronomical telescope		**1609** Ben Jonson, *Epicoene, or The Silent Woman*
1610 Henri IV of France assassinated; William Harvey discovers circulation of blood; Galileo observes Saturn for the first time		**1610** Ben Jonson, *The Alchemist*
	1611 Shakespeare's *Cymbeline*, *The Winter's Tale* and *The Tempest* performed	**1611** 'King James' Bible ('Authorised' version)
1612 Last burning of heretics in England		
	1613 Globe Theatre burns down	
		1614 Sir Walter Raleigh, *The History of the World*
	1616 Death of William Shakespeare (23 April)	
1618 Raleigh executed for treason; Thirty Years War begins in England		
		1622 Birth of French dramatist Molière

OTHER EDITIONS OF ROMEO AND JULIET

Romeo and Juliet, Penguin Popular Classics, 1994
> Much the cheapest edition available. It has a chronological list of
> Shakespeare's plays, a brief introduction, notes and glossary, and a most
> interesting reconstruction of an Elizabethan performance on the basis of
> the stage directions in both Q1 and Q2

J.A. Bryant, Jr, ed., *Romeo and Juliet*, The Signet Classic
Shakespeare, New English Library, 1964
> A useful introduction and glossaries on the same page as the text, which
> saves the reader having to refer to the back of the book. There is no
> commentary on the text, but there are helpful excerpts from critical
> studies of the play and a discussion of the text and sources

**CHECK
THE FILM**

In all, over 300
adaptations of
Shakespeare's plays
have been filmed
since the oldest
surviving footage of
the great actress
Sarah Bernhardt
appearing the duel
scene of *Hamlet* in
1890.

Brian Gibbons, ed., *Romeo and Juliet*, The Arden Shakespeare,
Routledge, 1980
> A scholarly edition, with a long introduction discussing the text, date,
> sources and literary qualities of the play, and very full notes on each page
> which explain vocabulary, allusions and points of detail

G. Blakemore, ed., *Romeo and Juliet*, New Cambridge Shakespeare,
Cambridge University Press, 1984
> Another scholarly edition which may be consulted on all textual and
> critical matters

Jill L. Stevenson, ed., *Romeo and Juliet*, The Oxford Shakespeare,
Oxford University Press, 2000
> A first-rate and up-to-date scholarly edition, with full introduction,
> notes and illustrations from stage and film productions of the play.
> Thoroughly recommended.

GENERAL WORKS

Ilana Krausman Ben-Amos, *Adolescence and Youth in Early Modern
England,* Yale University Press, 1994
> An illuminating study of attitudes to, and expectations of, young people,
> with relevance to the predicament of Romeo and Juliet.

G. Bullough, ed., *Narrative and Dramatic Sources of Shakespeare*, 8 vols., Routledge & Kegan Paul, 1957–75.
Volume 1 reprints Brooke's *Tragicall Hystorye*

Jonathan Dollimore, *Radical Tragedy: Religion, Ideology and Power in the drama of Shakespeare and his Contemporaries*, 2nd edn, Harvester, 1989
A cultural materialist account of Elizabethan drama as critically subversive

John Drakakis, ed., *Alternative Shakespeares*, New Accents, Methuen, 1985
A seminal collection of contemporary approaches to Shakespeare

— *Shakespearean Tragedy*, Longman Critical Readers 1992

A collection of contemporary theoretical approaches, with an essay on *Romeo and Juliet* by Julia Kristeva

Juliet Dusinberre, *Shakespeare and the Nature of Women*, Macmillan, 1975
An excellent introduction to the subject

Terry Eagleton, *William Shakespeare*, Blackwell, 1986
A lively and accessible account of Shakespeare in the light of deconstruction, feminism and Marxism

Charles Edelman, *Brawl Ridiculous: Swordfighting in Shakespeare's Plays*, Manchester University Press, 1992
Provides a cultural context for the violence in *Romeo and Juliet*

Michael Goldman, *Shakespeare and the Energies of Drama*, Princeton University Press, 1972
Interesting about the power of sexual desire in *Romeo and Juliet*

Andrew Gurr, *The Shakespearean Stage, 1574–1642*, 3rd edn, Cambridge University Press, 1992
The standard work on the subject

Andrew Gurr, *Playgoing in Shakespeare's London*, 2nd edition, Cambridge University Press, 1996
Assembles all the available evidence about the structure of the theatres of Shakespeare's time, the circumstances in which the plays were performed, and the composition of the audiences which watched them.

CHECK THE FILM
In 1954 Laurence Harvey and Susan Shentall starred in a film version of *Romeo and Juliet*, directed by Renato Castellani.

FURTHER READING

 CHECK THE NET

A Web search for 'Shakespeare' brings up nearly 4 million sites.

Lisa Jardine, *Still Harping on Daughters: women and drama in the age of Shakespeare*, Harvester, 1983
> A feminist account of notions about, and the depiction of, women in the Elizabethan age and in Shakespeare with many observations relevant to *Romeo and Juliet*

Murray J. Levith, *What's in Shakespeare's Names*, Allen and Unwin, 1978
> Explains the significance of the names of characters in Shakespeare's plays

M. M. Mahood, *Shakespeare's Wordplay*, Methuen, 1957
> Discusses Shakespeare's quibbles and puns

C.T. Onions, *A Shakespeare Glossary*, Oxford University Press, 1911 (frequently reprinted)
> Gives explanations of many of the difficult words and phrases in Shakespeare's plays

Eric Partridge, *Shakespeare's Bawdy,* Routledge, 1947 (frequently reprinted)
> The best source on Shakespeare's use of sexual imagery, puns, jokes and innuendo.

Kiernan Ryan, *Shakespeare*, 2nd edn, Harvester, 1995
> Surveys contemporary approaches to Shakespeare and has a section challenging traditional readings of *Romeo and Juliet*

S. Schoenbaum, *William Shakespeare: a Compact Documentary Life*, Clarendon Press, 1977
> The most authoritative biography

T.J.B. Spencer, ed., *Elizabethan Love Stories*, Penguin, 1968
> Reprints William Painter's version of *Rhomeo and Julietta*

Michael Spiller, *Early Modern Sonneteers*, Northcote House, 2001
> The most recent account of the Renaissance sonneteering vogue.

CRITICAL STUDIES OF *ROMEO AND JULIET*

John F. Andrews, ed., *Romeo and Juliet:: Critical Essays*, Garland, 1993
A very useful collection of essays on the play on a wide range of topics.

Nicholas Brooke, *Shakespeare's Early Tragedies*, Methuen, 1968
Discusses the patterning of the play in language and structure

J.R. Brown, and B. Harris, eds., *Early Shakespeare*, Stratford-upon-Avon Studies III, Arnold, 1961
Includes an essay by John Lawlor on *Romeo and Juliet* as a medieval tragedy

Dympna Callaghan, *Weyward Sisters: Shakespeare and Feminist Politics*, Blackwell, 1994
Contains her essay, ' The Ideology of Romantic Love', which comments on Act I.3. of *Romeo and Juliet*

Douglas Cole, ed., *Twentieth-century Interpretations of Romeo and Juliet*, Prentice-Hall, 1970
A collection of appreciative essays

Samuel Taylor Coleridge, *Shakespearean Criticism*, ed. T. M. Raysor, 2 vols, Dent, 1960
Includes a lecture and several passages on the play

Marjorie Kolb Cox, 'Adolescent Processes in *Romeo and Juliet*', *Psychoanalytical Review*, 63, 1976
Interesting on adolescent rivalry and passion in *Romeo and Juliet*

Franklin Dickey, *Not Wisely But Too Well: Shakespeare's Tragedies of Love*, Huntingdon Library, San Marino CA 1957
Ideas of love in the play seen as a Christian tragedy

John Drakakis, ed., *Shakespearian Tragedy*, Longman, 1992
Includes an essay by the French feminist Julia Kristeva on '*Romeo and Juliet:* Love-Hatred in the Couple'

> **CONTEXT**
> The British Library holds nearly 1.5 million books by or about Shakespeare.

FURTHER READING

Peter Erickson and Coppélia Kahn, eds, *Rough Magic: Renaissance Essays in Honor of C.L. Barber,* University of Delaware Press, 1985
Includes an essay by Edward Snow on ' Language and Sexual Difference in *Romeo and Juliet*'

CONTEXT

The most authoritative texts and fullest scholarly notes to individual plays by Shakespeare are those in the Arden series. First published by Methuen in the late nineteenth century a third edition began publication by Nelson in 1995.

Jonathan Goldberg, ed., *Queering the Renaissance*, Duke University Press, 1994
Includes an essay by Goldberg on same-sex attraction and homo-eroticism in *Romeo and Juliet*

H. Granville Barker, *Prefaces to Shakespeare*, 2 vols, Batsford, 1958
Especially good on how the play might best be presented in the theatre

A.C. Hamilton, *The Early Shakespeare*, Huntington Library, 1967
The play in relation to the comedies

G.B. Harrison, *Shakespeare's Tragedies*, Routledge, 1951
A very useful introductory essay

Coppélia Kahn, *Man's Estate: Masculine Identity in Shakespeare*, University of California Press, 1981
In a chapter on marriage and manhood in *Romeo and Juliet* and *The Taming of the Shrew*, the author discusses adolescent relationships and rites of passage to maturity

L. Lerner, ed., *Shakespeare's Tragedies: An Anthology of Modern Criticism*, Penguin, 1963
Includes extracts from M.M. Mahood, *Shakespeare's Wordplay*, London, 1957, an excellent discussion of the quibbling and punning in the play, and C. Williams, *The English Poetic Mind*, London, 1932

Carolyn Ruth Swift Lenz, Gayle Greene and Carol Thomas Neely, eds, *The Woman's Part: Feminist Criticism of Shakespeare*, Urbana, Ill., 1983
Includes a fine essay by Coppélia Kahn on youth, gender and patriarchal power structures in the play, entitled 'Coming of Age in Verona'

James N. Loehlin, ed., *Romeo and Juliet*, Shakespeare in Production series, Cambridge University Press, 2002
A survey of changing styles in the production of the play

H.A. Mason, *Shakespeare's Tragedies of Love*, Chatto and Windus, 1970

Discusses particularly the relationship between Shakespeare's treatment of love and the tragedy

O.H. Moore, *The Legend of Romeo and Juliet*, Ohio State University Press, 1950

A full account of the development of the Romeo and Juliet story

Joseph A. Porter, *Shakespeare's Mercutio: his History and Drama*, University of North Carolina Press, 1988

A book-length account of this character from *Romeo and Juliet*

Sasha Robert, *Romeo and Juliet*, Northcote House, 1998

A good brief introduction to the play in the Writers and their Work series

Leah Scragg, *Shakespeare's Mouldy Tales*, Longman, 1992

Accessible discussion of Shakespeare's manipulation of his sources, with a section on *Romeo and Juliet*

E.E. Stoll, *Shakespeare's Young Lovers*, Oxford University Press, 1937

A fine essay on the characters of Romeo and Juliet and the nature of their love

Neil Taylor and Bryan Loughrey, eds, *Shakespeare's Early Tragedies: Richard III, Titus Andronicus and Romeo and Juliet*, Macmillan 1990

A useful collection of essays

J. Vyvyan, *Shakespeare and the Rose of Love*, Chatto & Windus, 1968

Ideas of love in the play

Cedric Watts, *Romeo and Juliet*, Harvester New Critical Introductions, Harvester, 1991

An excellent account of the play, paying particular attention to its sexual politics and to the interplay of lyricism and bawdy in its dramatisation of love

 CHECK THE NET

A Web search will find many sites devoted to proving Shakespeare's plays were the work of other writers (notably Christopher Marlowe or Francis Bacon).

CONTEXT

When, on 1 March 1662, the diarist Samuel Pepys saw the first production of *Romeo and Juliet* since the Restoration, he thought 'the play of itself the worst that ever I heard in my life, and the worst acted that ever I saw.'

LITERARY TERMS

blank verse unrhymed lines of five stresses (**iambic pentameter**)

conceit extended image

couplet a pair of rhymed lines

crux textual passage which puzzles commentators

Elizabethan wit clever inventiveness, ingenious dexterity with words, all containing the idea of surprise and unexpectedness

hyperbole emphasis by exaggeration

iambic pentameter a line of five stresses

irony saying one thing while meaning another; **tragic/dramatic irony** occurs when the audience knows more than the play's characters and can foresee the outcome

metaphor figure of speech in which something is spoken of as *being* that which it resembles

multivocal speaking with more than one voice

multivalent having more than one meaning

oxymoron combination of words of opposite meanings

parody an imitation of a style or work of literature designed to ridicule the original

Petrarch fourteenth-century Italian poet who gave his name to **Petrarchan (or courtly) love**, which idealised womanhood, and the **Petrarchan sonnet** (see **sonnet**)

quarto book made up of paper sheets folded to make four leaves

quatrain a stanza of four lines

self-reflexive plays that comment upon themselves as dramatic pieces

soliloquy a speech delivered by a character when alone, enabling him or her to reveal innermost thoughts and motivations

sonnet lyric poem consisting of fourteen rhyming lines of **iambic pentameter**; Elizabethan/Shakespearian sonnet, usually rhyming *abab cdcd efef gg*; Petrarchan sonnet, *abba abba cdd cdd* or *cde cde*

verisimilitude likeness to reality

Professor N.H. Keeble is currently Professor of English Studies at the University of Stirling, where he has taught for twenty years. During this time he has regularly run courses on Shakespeare. His research lies in the early modern period and he has published widely on English literature of the sixteenth and seventeenth centuries.

General editor

Martin Gray, former Head of the Department of English Studies at the University of Stirling, and of Literary Studies at the University of Luton.

Maya Angelou
I Know Why the Caged Bird Sings

Jane Austen
Pride and Prejudice

Alan Ayckbourn
Absent Friends

Elizabeth Barrett Browning
Selected Poems

Robert Bolt
A Man for All Seasons

Harold Brighouse
Hobson's Choice

Charlotte Brontë
Jane Eyre

Emily Brontë
Wuthering Heights

Shelagh Delaney
A Taste of Honey

Charles Dickens
David Copperfield
Great Expectations
Hard Times
Oliver Twist

Roddy Doyle
Paddy Clarke Ha Ha Ha

George Eliot
Silas Marner
The Mill on the Floss

Anne Frank
The Diary of a Young Girl

William Golding
Lord of the Flies

Oliver Goldsmith
She Stoops to Conquer

Willis Hall
The Long and the Short and the Tall

Thomas Hardy
Far from the Madding Crowd
The Mayor of Casterbridge
Tess of the d'Urbervilles
The Withered Arm and other Wessex Tales

L.P. Hartley
The Go-Between

Seamus Heaney
Selected Poems

Susan Hill
I'm the King of the Castle

Barry Hines
A Kestrel for a Knave

Louise Lawrence
Children of the Dust

Harper Lee
To Kill a Mockingbird

Laurie Lee
Cider with Rosie

Arthur Miller
The Crucible
A View from the Bridge

Robert O'Brien
Z for Zachariah

Frank O'Connor
My Oedipus Complex and Other Stories

George Orwell
Animal Farm

J.B. Priestley
An Inspector Calls
When We Are Married

Willy Russell
Educating Rita
Our Day Out

J.D. Salinger
The Catcher in the Rye

William Shakespeare
Henry IV Part I
Henry V
Julius Caesar
Macbeth
The Merchant of Venice
A Midsummer Night's Dream
Much Ado About Nothing
Romeo and Juliet
The Tempest
Twelfth Night

George Bernard Shaw
Pygmalion

Mary Shelley
Frankenstein

R.C. Sherriff
Journey's End

Rukshana Smith
Salt on the snow

John Steinbeck
Of Mice and Men

Robert Louis Stevenson
Dr Jekyll and Mr Hyde

Jonathan Swift
Gulliver's Travels

Robert Swindells
Daz 4 Zoe

Mildred D. Taylor
Roll of Thunder, Hear My Cry

Mark Twain
Huckleberry Finn

James Watson
Talking in Whispers

Edith Wharton
Ethan Frome

William Wordsworth
Selected Poems

A Choice of Poets

Mystery Stories of the Nineteenth Century including The Signalman

Nineteenth Century Short Stories

Poetry of the First World War

Six Women Poets

For the AQA Anthology:

Duffy and Armitage & Pre-1914 Poetry

Heaney and Clarke & Pre-1914 Poetry

Poems from Different Cultures